ISSUES THAT CONCERN YOU

Social Networking

Daniel Gaetán-Beltrán, *Book Editor*

GREENHAVEN PRESS
A part of Gale, Cengage Learning

Farmington Hills, Mich • San Francisco • New York • Waterville, Maine
Meriden, Conn • Mason, Ohio • Chicago

Patricia Coryell, *Vice President & Publisher, New Products & GVRL*
Douglas Dentino, *Manager, New Products*
Judy Galens, *Acquisitions Editor*

© 2015 Greenhaven Press, a part of Gale, Cengage Learning

WCN: 01-100-101

Articles in Greenhaven Press anthologies are often edited for length to meet page requirements. In addition, original titles of these works are changed to clearly present the main thesis and to explicitly indicate the author's opinion. Every effort is made to ensure that Greenhaven Press accurately reflects the original intent of the authors. Every effort has been made to trace the owners of copyrighted material.

Cover image © Szasz-Fabian Jozsef/Shutterstock.com

LIBRARY OF CONGRESS CATALOGING-IN-PUBLICATION DATA

Social networking / Daniel Gaetán-Beltrán, book editor.
   pages cm. -- (Issues that concern you)
   Includes bibliographical references and index.
   ISBN 978-0-7377-7240-1 (hardcover)
   1. Online social networks. 2. Social networks. 3. Social media. I. Gaetán-Beltrán, Daniel.
   HM742.S6295 2015
   302.30285--dc23
                                                                   2014040689

Printed in the United States of America
1 2 3 4 5 6 7 19 18 17 16 15

CONTENTS

Facebook is a behemoth and a true phenomenon. About 11 percent of the world's population and 71 percent of adults who are online are on Facebook, and it is currently the leading social networking site, ranked by number of users. But it did not all start with Facebook. The history of social networking can be traced back almost to the very beginnings of the Internet itself. Fewer than ten years after computers started to be connected with each other via telephone lines, the first simple computer tool for sharing information with friends was created. It was called a bulletin board system (BBS), and computer hobbyists in Chicago started the first one in 1978. A year later, a BBS connected Duke University with the University of North Carolina at Chapel Hill. Social networking is part of the virtual DNA of the complex computer networks that we know as the Internet.

Individuals started creating personal websites as early as 1994, when a service called Geocities began providing tools and hosting services for user-created sites. In just a few years, the first social networking sites began to emerge and spread. In 1999, Friends Reunited, the first social network to achieve prominence, was founded in Great Britain. It was quickly followed by Friendster in 2002 and MySpace and LinkedIn in 2003. A year later, students at Harvard University created Facebook as a school version of Friendster. YouTube emerged in 2005 and Twitter in 2006. Services for sharing images and short videos and personal postings continue to proliferate a decade later. Today, other well-known networks include Blogger, Flickr, Instagram, LiveJournal, Lulu, Pinterest, Reddit, Second Life, Snapchat, Typepad, Wetpaint, Wikidot, Wikipedia, and WordPress.

Social networking is popular because it fulfills a basic human need: to connect with others. Millions of people throughout the world use social networking to meet others and share information and experiences. Social networking tools allow people—strangers, family, friends, enemies—to share almost anything: questions and answers to problems, recipes, professional tips, photos, videos, essays, songs. By definition, the content of social networking sites is created by their community users, rather than by a single person or institutional creator. So, the range of topics that unite users online is nearly infinite, limited only by what may interest any two people. Wikipedia currently lists 206 online social networks—and warns that its list is not exhaustive. Some networks focus on very specific interests; however, the networks with which most people are familiar (e.g., Facebook and Twitter) have open memberships and are available to anyone who wants to join.

Social networking can be useful, entertaining, and pleasurable. In fact, most teens report positive outcomes when asked about their experiences on social media. Young people in the United States have a wide array of social networking apps that allow them to communicate, share files, video-chat, and shop. These tools help them maintain school and family relationships, make new friends, and display their creativity. Twitter is popular for its brief message posts used to share quick facts or thoughts as well as keep up with events locally and around the world. A number of social networking services are centered on the sharing of photos and videos. With Instagram, teens can quickly share very short videos or customize photos with arty filters. On Snapchat, the short videos or photos disappear after a short amount of time. Vine, which is owned by Twitter, allows users to create six-second video loops. These are only some of the more established and popular sites. Newer social networking sites that also have proved to be popular with teens include Wanelo, Kik Messenger, Oovoo, Yik Yak, Omegle, Yo, and Whisper.

As social networking's popularity has increased, so have questions about safety and privacy online, especially for young people. Alarmingly, many people on social media do not understand or use privacy settings, leaving themselves vulnerable to privacy violations. More important, everything a user puts online is potentially there forever (even Snapchat posts). Young people can be particularly vulnerable as they apply to college or look for jobs.

A comment or photo that was funny or interesting at the time may be less so months or years later when scrutinized by a college admissions officer or potential employer.

In recent years, social networking has become closely associated with the desire to do good and make the world a better place. A wave of demonstrations and protests in the Middle East from 2010 to around 2013 was fueled in large part by the effective use of social media. The men and women seeking political change tended to be young, and young people throughout the world have been the earliest adopters of social media. This period in the Middle East has come to be known as the Arab Spring, and the movements it sparked are sometimes called "Twitter revolutions." In a number of countries—including Tunisia, Egypt, and Libya—social networking services, particularly Facebook and Twitter, were used to organize and share information. Social networking was also effectively used to raise awareness internationally about political and social issues in these countries.

Also of note have been social awareness campaigns conducted on social media. A prime example is *Kony2012*. The group Invisible Children created this short film to raise awareness of the atrocities committed by cult military leader Joseph Kony and the Lord's Resistance Army in a number of countries in central Africa. The campaign went "viral"; that is, became extremely popular through the process of being shared on social media. For a number of years it was considered the most viral video ever, having reached 100 million views worldwide in only six days. The campaign is credited with spurring a US Senate resolution condemning Kony and with encouraging the deployment of African Union troops to apprehend him. But such cyberactivism—deemed slacktivism by critics—has also been condemned as a poor substitute for real-world involvement and true commitment to social or political change.

Social networking can have both positive and negative effects. It can be used for social and political change as well as to give voice to shameless narcissism. People's increasing reliance on social networking and technology for communication is often criticized. Some commentators argue that it impairs people's ability to socialize in real life. Others are concerned that social media enables harassment, bullying, and even sexual assault. Some critics point out that young girls and LGBT (lesbian, gay, bisexual, and transgender) youth are particularly vulnerable on social media. The viewpoints in *Issues That Concern You: Social Networking* explore these and other important issues related to social media in the contemporary life of teens.

ONE

The Upside of Selfies: Social Media Isn't All Bad for Kids

Kelly Wallace

In the following viewpoint a journalist reviews the benefits of social networking for teens. The author begins by acknowledging that, as a parent, she is keenly aware of the negative aspects and dangers of social media; however, she cites research and anecdotes that illustrate the good side of social networking for young people. For example, she writes that social networking can be an outlet for isolated teens and that social media sites can encourage social activism. Teens themselves feel that social networking improves their lives, according to research the author cites. Overall, she writes, teens are able to do just fine in the world of social networking. Kelly Wallace is a digital correspondent and editor at large at the Cable News Network (CNN), covering family life and career issues.

I'll admit it right at the start: When I think about teens and social media, I immediately begin to tally up the negatives.

What good could possibly come from teens and tweens spending gobs of time on online networks, posting nonstop "selfies," some in rather suggestive poses, and often communicating with people they don't even know?

A running joke at home: My girls, ages 6 and 7, can't get iPhones until they're 40.

Most Young People Use Social Networking Sites

Social networking site use by age group, 2005–2013. Percent of Internet users in each age group who use social networking sites, over time.

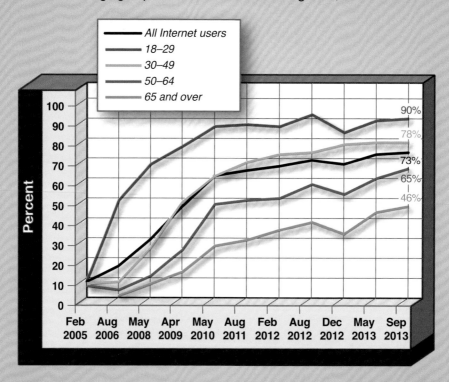

Note: Latest data from Pew Research Center's Inernet Project Library Survey, July 19–September 30, 2013. N = 5,112 Internet users ages 18 and over. Interviews were conducted in English and Spanish and on landline and cell phones. The margin of error for results based on Internet users is +/- 1.6 percentage points.

Taken from: Pew Research Center Internet Project, "Social Networking Fact Sheet," January 2014. www.pewinternet.org.

But then I chat with other moms, who always know best, and a picture emerges that social media is not always the scary enemy some of us might think it is for our tweens and teens.

Take the "selfie," for example, which if you haven't already heard has been named Oxford Dictionaries' word of the year for 2013. Really!

Eileen Masio, a mom of two in New York, monitors her daughter Amelia's Instagram account 24/7. Yes, most of the posts are "selfies," but it's the comments that make her think there is also a positive to this nonstop engagement.

"I think just as damaging as social media can be, it can . . . help to build self-confidence, too," said Masio, during a recent interview including her husband, 13-year-old Amelia and 8-year-old son William.

"When they post selfies, all the comments I usually see are 'You're beautiful,' 'You're so pretty,' 'Oh my God, gorgeous,'" said Masio.

Teens See Positive Aspects of Social Media

In fact, according to a report last year [2012] by the nonprofit child advocacy group Common Sense Media, one in five [20%] teens said social media makes them feel more confident, compared with 4% who said it makes them feel less so.

In the survey of more than 1,000 13- to 17-year-olds about how they view their digital lives, 28% said social networking made them feel more outgoing versus 5% who said it made them feel less so; and 29% said it made them feel less shy versus the 3% who said it made them feel more introverted.

When it comes to relationships with friends, more than half (52%) of teens said social media has made them better versus just 4% who said it has negatively affected those relationships.

"On the whole, teens said that they feel that social media has a more positive than negative impact on their social and emotional lives," said Shira Lee Katz, Common Sense Media's director of digital media. "They believe that social media helps their friendships, makes them feel more outgoing and gives them confidence."

News Outlets Focus on the Negative

The findings are likely to come as a surprise to most parents, including this writer, especially because most of what we hear about social media, especially *in* the media, are the negatives, such as how cyberbullying can turn tragic.

"For every heartbreaking case of cyberbullying, there are many stories of teens using social media for good," said Katz.

Rebecca Levey, cofounder of a video sharing platform for tweens ages 7 to 12 called KidzVuz, has seen it firsthand. During a special partnership with the Tony Awards earlier this year, kids were encouraged to either make videos singing parts of their favorite show tunes or talk about why theater was so important to them.

"The response from other kids was so awesome. I mean we had kids who were truly tone deaf and it didn't matter," said Levey with a chuckle. "Everyone's like, 'You're awesome,' 'Go follow your dream,' 'Don't give up.'"

Levey said another benefit is for kids who might feel slightly isolated to connect with other tweens and teens who share their same interests.

"They can just find other kids who are super excited about the same thing, so if you are living in a small town and you're the only kid who loves musical theater, instead of feeling like a freak about it, you can go online and find all these other kids that love musical theater," she said.

Social media has been a place where teens, who might be feeling isolated, can cry for help. For example, when an 18-year-old recently posted on his Facebook page that he was thinking of jumping off the George Washington Bridge, which connects New York with New Jersey, Port Authority officers managed to connect with him on social media and encouraged him to get help.

Teens Use Social Media for Social Good

Teens have also shown they can use social media to make their voices heard. After a Christian motivational speaker, who believes "dateable girls know how to shut up," spoke at a high school in Richardson, Texas, students took to Twitter to express their outrage.

A group of teens takes a selfie to post online. Many teens believe that participation in social networking sites helps with self-esteem and a sense of belonging.

One student wrote on Twitter, "Don't you guys just love listening to sexist comments, irrational comparisons and blunt stereotypes w/o actual proof or evidence?"

"Teens and this young generation in general want action," said Elena Sonnino, a founder of the site Live.Do.Grow, social media strategist and writer who focuses on engaging tweens and teens in using their voice for social good.

"They want to be able to see, for better or for worse, really quick action and social media allows them to create positive, meaningful change quickly."

Sonnino, who has created a Facebook group called Grow Global Citizens, said social media has not only increased tweens and teens' awareness of the world around them, but also has allowed them to be more innovative about how they can get involved.

"In the past . . . they would do canned food drives, they'd do the book drives, they'd do all the things that have been done over and over, which were all wonderful, don't get me wrong, but now . . . they're realizing there is so much more they can do," said Sonnino.

At a recent digital family summit, Sonnino said she heard from kids who are doing things like creating Rainbow Loom bracelets to raise money for cystic fibrosis, and taking "selfies" and using the hashtag #unselfie to promote awareness of "Giving Tuesday," the Tuesday after Thanksgiving, which is billed as a day to promote giving to others during the holiday season.

The Parents' Role

Levey said she and KidzVuz cofounder Nancy Friedman try to urge parents to, in essence, get with the program about social media. The genie is out of the bottle, folks.

"We liken it to the sex talks," said Levey. "You can either have the argument that you never want to tell your kids about sex and you don't want them to learn, and then good luck to them, or you can give them the rules and sort of be there with them every step of the way."

"I think part of the problem is parents, unlike (talking about) sex, really don't know the rules themselves," she said.

But teens like Amelia Masio are learning the digital ropes and are showing us parents that they're just fine in the vast social media landscape.

Recently, Amelia stood up for someone who was being criticized online, and viewed the exchange "kind of like math in a way, with negative and positive positions."

"If one person says this thing, it brings them down, but if this (other) person says the equal amount just as good, it evens out to a zero," she said.

I'm feeling better already!

TWO

Social Networking Impairs the Ability to Socialize in Real Life

Jacqueline Olds

In the following viewpoint, Jacqueline Olds discusses the book *Alone Together: Why We Expect More from Technology and Less from Each Other* by social scientist Sherry Turkle. The author explains that Turkle is a technology expert who has become concerned about the reliance on electronic devices for communication. Turkle's book, Olds explains, details how new technologies affect how people communicate and how young people learn and develop interpersonal skills. The new technology makes it possible to communicate short and clipped bits of information and to be connected to friends and colleagues in real time. These tools for social networking, however, are also changing how family members interact and relate to each other, the author notes. Jacqueline Olds is associate clinical professor of psychiatry at Harvard Medical School. She teaches child and adult psychiatry at the McLean and Massachusetts General hospitals and has a private psychiatry practice in Cambridge, Massachusetts.

Sherry Turkle, in her new book *Alone Together: Why We Expect More from Technology and Less from Each Other*, argues that humans are at a "robotic moment" in history. People have reached a "state of emotional—and I would say philosophical—readiness," she writes, in which they are "willing to seriously consider robots not only as pets but as potential friends, confidants, and even romantic partners."

To make her case, Turkle first discusses people's responses to actual robots. Part one of the book, "The Robotic Moment: In Solitude, New Intimacies," begins with ELIZA, the computer program created by Joseph Weizenbaum at MIT [Massachusetts Institure of Technology] in the 1960s that "conversed" with people via text on the screen, mimicking psychotherapeutic dialogue, and quickly moves to robotic "pets." She reports the results of interviews she conducted with children about their interactions with Tamagotchis, tiny toys first released in 1997 that appear on a screen housed in a plastic egg and "ask" their owners to take care of them. She analyses the results of similar studies with the Furby, a hamsterlike robot popular among children and adults in the late 1990s; the AIBO, a robotic "dog" released in 1999; and My Real Baby, a robotic doll released in 2000. These toys have unpredictable responses to their child owners, leading to confused responses and much theorizing by the children about whether and how the toys are alive or dead, real or fake. Children's concepts about what makes something alive, she writes, have evolved since the 1970s to center on "an object's seeming potential for mutual care." This, Turkle suggests, is one hallmark of the "robotic moment." Turkle has also studied robots created for people who are nearing the end of their lives. She notes that many people are persuaded that they will be better off and less of a burden if they let robots take care of them as they age, rather than letting humans do their expensive and often inadequate caretaking.

Concerns About Electronic Devices

But Turkle points out that her book is not just about robots: "Rather, it is about how we are changed as technology offers us substitutes for connecting with each other face to face." Part two of the book, "Networked: In Intimacy; New Solitudes," moves from the more literal examples robots offer to the subtleties of online communication, text messaging and online gaming communities such as Second Life, whose users can craft their online identities and appearances and build homes and businesses within the game. Turkle's careful description of what she says are still the "early days" of the Internet displays both her curiosity and her concern about the effects of technology. She interviews people who seem more taken with their robot friends, cell phones and computers than are most people I can think of. In fact, I found

Sherry Turkle, a technology expert at the Massachusetts Institute of Technology, is concerned about how reliance on electronic devices may affect personal relationships.

many of the interview subjects' attachment to these devices quite surprising. Still, these people aren't so far off from the people I know that her arguments seem completely implausible—and the points Turkle makes are important ones.

Turkle's conclusions are based on years of research exploring people's interactions with and responses to electronic devices. This includes a number of studies she has conducted herself, many of which entailed interviewing elementary-school students, college students and adults about their use of technology. Hers is clearly an effort to report results evenhandedly. Still, reading her analysis, I sense that she feels we might all have sold ourselves down the river to technology that was supposed to save us time and leave us more available for the activities and intimacies that really matter to us. She argues, as have many others, that we are dominated by our cell phones, computers, e-mails and text messages, rather than controlling our use of them to increase our efficiency and thus our free time. She doesn't like to label excessive use of these devices as addiction—she writes, "To combat addiction, you have to discard the addicting substance. But we are not going to 'get rid' of the Internet." But she thinks, and in this I completely agree with her, that "we have to find a way to live with seductive technology and make it work to our purposes."

Alone Together is the final book in a trilogy that began with Turkle's 1984 book *The Second Self* and continued in *Life on the Screen*, which was published in 1995. This latest book represents something of a shift—Turkle was more optimistic about the role of technology earlier in her career. And the changes in her thinking have yielded some compelling arguments. One of these is Turkle's exploration of how confusing it is for young children to be confronted with robotic toys that respond to them in complex, humanlike "voices" and express needs and feelings. Part of what child psychiatrists appreciate about inanimate toys is that children get to write the script for make-believe play using the toys to work out issues in their own development. Play is not quite as creative when someone has programmed a randomized script into a toy that purports to have feelings of its own.

"You'll have to excuse me. I'm not used to talking to people, in real-time, without using a mobile device."

"You'll have to excuse me. I'm not used to talking to people, in real-time, without using a mobile device," cartoon by Marty Bucella, www.CartoonStock.com. Copyright © Marty Bucella. Reproduction rights obtainable from www.CartoonStock.com.

Technology and Social Communication Among Teens

Turkle writes, unsurprisingly, that young people depend too much on instant messaging and text messaging as a way of conducting friendships. And indeed, we now know from neuroscience research that there are areas in the prefrontal cortex that determine the development of social judgment, and that these areas rely on input from all five senses (and the internal organs) in order to help us make decisions about what would be an appropriate response to a situation. When children and teenagers communicate via the typed word as they learn about human interactions and friendships, they don't develop the skills of friendship or the sound social judgment that they would if they had face-to-face contact the way they did in the past. Luckily school isn't conducted online yet, so children still get to practice peer interchange for a few hours of every day. On a more optimistic note, she persuasively quotes some teenagers who have recognized the way in which face-to-face connections are superior to sending text messages and e-mails or using Skype to make video calls. They are trying to put aside their curiosity about their next important message and devote time to their close friends without the interference of technology. But I was dismayed to read that many of these teenagers say their parents can't concentrate on actual conversations in the present moment because they are reading e-mails on their BlackBerries.

Turkle details how successive new technologies have changed how we communicate, noting how much information is conveyed by the human voice as transmitted by the telephone and how rare and lovely the sound of another's voice is. But we got tired of phone calls, so many of us switched to e-mails or voice mails (designed so we wouldn't have to encounter someone directly by phone). I would add that these communication fads play out in the realm of family dynamics. In their efforts to avoid adults' scrutiny, teenagers take the lead in adopting new methods of technological communication, sending text messages rather than leaving voice mails, for instance. Adults end up following suit because they want to be aware of what their children are doing. But with each new technology, the messages become more clipped and contain less information, sometimes losing subtlety along the way. We can only hope that the next technological leap won't require us to use only our thumbs—or even less.

The Effect on Family Life

Although Turkle doesn't make this point, I think it's important to note that the evolution of communication technologies has happened in parallel with the move toward families with two full-time working parents. When middle- and upper-class women were less likely to have full-time jobs and more likely to have children, they spent more time watching their children play, shopping, visiting with friends and keeping track of the whereabouts of their families. As more and more women began to choose to have careers, communication technologies were becoming more advanced. Catalog shopping, marketed to working women, was one of the harbingers of this change. Along with telephones, which made it easier to keep in touch, these and other developments established technology as an essential part of maintaining one's home and family. And as some of the men who were these women's partners slowly adopted a more equal share of work in the home, they too became more pressed for time. Now computers, cell phones and text messages have become ways of keeping track of children, spouses, relatives and friends. And once it's possible to be in communication with one's family all the time, it's easy to feel guilty or worried if that connection is ever broken. Meanwhile, children realize they are being closely monitored—a phenomenon Turkle notes—and valiantly attempt to get distance from their parents and closer contact with their friends, even if that contact comes in the form of online video games and text messages. So along with technological changes, fear and its close companion, guilt, have helped to bang us to this peculiar state of affairs. *Alone Together* sheds new light on the situation.

Even though, to my mind, Turkle seems to have an uncanny knack for finding interview subjects who are putting too much store in their electronic devices, her ideas about the state we've come to—in which people sometimes prefer presenting a made-up self online rather than a real self in person—are important and deserve attention. In a different era, we would have worried that people who stayed in their fantasies to the extent that some computer users do were headed toward schizophrenia. If we're now prepared to believe that time spent with computers is a reasonable alternative to real relationships, we definitely need a correction in course! Thanks to Turkle's carefully researched book, we may be drawing closer to that correction.

THREE

Social Media Create New Challenges for Teens

danah boyd

The author of the following viewpoint, danah boyd, studies how young people use social networking technology in their daily lives. In the course of her research, she has discussed personal experiences on social media with many teens, covering topics such as identity, privacy, safety, danger, and bullying. In this viewpoint, she notes that teens make their own rules for expressing themselves on social media. She explains that some online behavior that seems inappropriate—the use of fake information on profiles, for example—is part of how teens craft their personal identities within a social group. She compares online postings to the decorative accessories in a teen's bedroom: items that help define a virtual space where one can hang out with friends. A key problem, boyd points out, is that teens' online space can inadvertently "collide" with other social spheres (school or church, for example). What is funny and appropriate among friends may be less so when shared with people outside the group. Therefore, teens should be aware of the potential consequences of material posted on social media. A principal researcher at Microsoft Research, danah boyd is also a research assistant professor in media, culture, and communication at New York University and a fellow at Harvard University's Berkman Center for Internet and Society.

Many teens post information on social media that they think is funny or intended to give a particular impression to a narrow audience without considering how this same content might be read out of context. Much of what seems like inaccurate identity information is simply a misinterpretation of a particular act of self-presentation. This issue was particularly noticeable in early social media genres in which explicit identity information was required for participation. Consider, for example, MySpace, which required a user to provide age, sex, location, and other fields to create a profile. . . . I met many teens who fabricated answers like name, location, age, and income to profile questions. They thought it was amusing to indicate their relationship status on Facebook as "It's Complicated" whether they were in a relationship or not. A casual viewer scanning Facebook might conclude that an extraordinary number of teens are in same-sex relationships because so many have chosen to list their best friend as the person that they are "In a Relationship" with. In the same vein, Facebook profiles suggest that the US census data must be inaccurate because, at least on Facebook, teens often have dozens of siblings; of course, a little bit of prying makes it clear that these, too, are close friends. These are but a few of the playful ways in which teens responded to social media sites' requests for information by providing inaccurate information that actually contains meaningful signals about friendship and sociality.

When I talked with teens, I learned that there were also numerous ways of repurposing social network site fields for entertainment and humor. Outside of wealthy communities, where talking about money is deemed gauche, I met countless teens who told MySpace that their income was "$250,000+." Choosing a birth year that made the age field depict "69" was also a common, if unsurprising, trend among teenage boys. Searching for social media users in Afghanistan or Zimbabwe offers an additional window into teen life, as many teens select the top or bottom choice in the

Perceived Effect of Social Networking on Social and Emotional Well-Being

Among the 75 percent of 13- to 17-year-olds with a social networking profile, percent who say social networking makes them feel more or less:

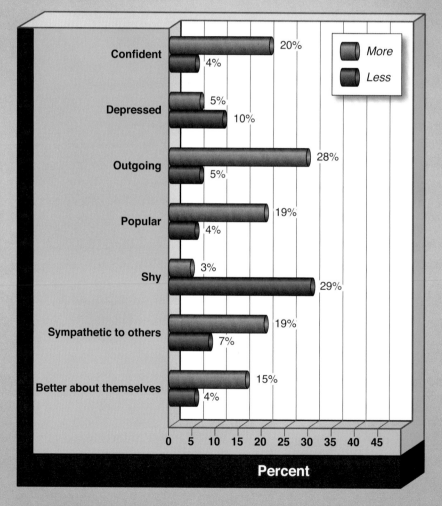

Category	More	Less
Confident	20%	4%
Depressed	5%	10%
Outgoing	28%	5%
Popular	19%	4%
Shy	3%	29%
Sympathetic to others	19%	7%
Better about themselves	15%	4%

Percent

pull-down menu when they indicate their location. Facebook expected users to provide "real names," but many teens I met offered up only their first name, preferring to select a last name of a celebrity, fictional character, or friend. These were but a few of the ways that teens provided what appeared to be fictitious information on their profiles. These practices allowed them to feel control over their profiles, particularly given how often they told me that it was ridiculous for sites to demand this information.

Teens' Own Rules for Social Media Profiles

One way of reading teens' profiles is to assume that they are lying. But marking oneself as rich or from a foreign land is not about deception; it's a simple way to provide entertaining signals to friends while ignoring a site's expectations. Most teens aren't enacting an imagined identity in a virtual world. Instead, they're simply refusing to play by the rules of self-presentation as defined by these sites. They see no reason to provide accurate information, in part because they know that most people who are reading what they post already know who they are. As Dominic, a white sixteen-year-old from Seattle, told me, he doesn't have to provide accurate information "because all my [social media] friends are actually my friends; they'll know if I'm joking around or not." Awareness of the social context helps shape what teens share and don't share. Many teens treat social media requests for information as a recommendation, not a requirement, because they view these sites purely as platforms for interacting with classmates and other people they know from other settings.

Why teens share what they do is neither arbitrary nor dictated by the social media sites where they hang out—nor by the norms that govern adults' use of those same sites. The youth-oriented social context in which teens share matters. Teens don't see social media as a virtual space in which they must choose to be themselves or create an alternate ego. They see social media as a place to gather with friends while balancing privacy and safety with humor and image. When Los Angeles–based Chicano fifteen-year-old Mickey says, "It's not that I lie on [MySpace], but I don't put my real information," he's highlighting that his choice to provide false data allows him to control the social situation. He doesn't want to be easily searchable by his parents or teachers, nor does he want to be found by "creeps" who might be browsing the site looking for vulnerable teenagers. He wants to be in a space with friends, and so he provides just enough information that his friends can find him without increasing his visibility to adults.

Teens fabricate information because it's funny, because they believe that the site has no reason to ask, or because they believe that doing so will limit their visibility to people they don't want to find them. In doing so, they are seeking to control the networked social context.

When teens create profiles through social media, they are simultaneously navigating extraordinarily public environments and more intimate friendship spaces. Media scholars Paul Hodkinson and Siân Lincoln argue that constructing these profiles can be understood through the lens of "bedroom culture." Just as many middle-class teens use different media artifacts—including photographs, posters, and tchotchkes—to personalize their bedrooms, teens often decorate their online self-presentations using a variety of media. Likewise, teens use their bedrooms to create a space for hanging out with friends and they turn to social media to do the same online. Yet because of the properties of social media, creating boundaries around these online spaces is far more difficult. Although teens complain about the impossibility of keeping siblings and parents out of their rooms, achieving privacy in social media is even harder. This, in turn, challenges teens' ability to meaningfully portray the nuances of who they are to different and conflicting audiences.

Self-Presentation in Social Media

In *The Presentation of Self in Everyday Life*, sociologist Erving Goffman describes the social rituals involved in self-presentation as "impression management." He argues that the impressions we make on others are a product of what is *given* and what is *given off*. In other words, what we convey to others is a matter of what we choose to share in order to make a good impression and also what we unintentionally reveal as a byproduct of who we are and how we react to others. The norms, cultural dynamics, and institutions where giving and giving off happen help define the broader context of how these performances are understood. When interpreting others' self-presentations, we read the explicit content that is conveyed in light of the implicit information that is given off and the context in which everything takes place. The tension between the explicit and implicit signals allows us to obtain much richer information about individuals' attempts to shape how

Social media allows teens to create online identities using information about themselves that may be inaccurate.

they're perceived. Of course, our reactions to their attempts to impress us enable them to adjust what they give in an attempt to convey what they think is best.

Based on their understanding of the social situation—including the context and the audience—people make decisions about what to share in order to act appropriately for the situation and to be perceived in the best light. When young people are trying to get a sense of the context in which they're operating, they're doing so in order to navigate the social situation in front of them. They may want to be seen as cool among their peers, even if adults would deem their behavior inappropriate. Teens may be trying to determine if someone they're attracted to is interested in them without embarrassing themselves. Or they may wish to be viewed as confident and happy, even when they're facing serious depression or anxiety. Whatever they're trying to convey, they must first get a grasp of the situation and the boundaries of the context. When contexts collapse or when information is taken out of context, teens can fail to make their intended impression.

Self-presentations are never constructed in a void. Goffman writes at length about the role individuals play in shaping their self-presentations, but he also highlights ways in which individuals are part of broader collectives that convey impressions about the whole group. In discussing the importance of "teams" for impression management, he points out that people work together to shape impressions, often relying on shared familiarity to help define any given situation in a mutually agreeable manner. He also argues that, "any member of the team has the power to give the show away or to disrupt it by inappropriate conduct." When teens create profiles online, they're both individuals and part of a collective. Their self-representation is constructed through what they explicitly provide, through what their friends share, and as a product of how other people respond to them. When Alice's friend Bob comments on her profile, he's affecting her self-presentation. Even the photo that Bob chooses as his primary photo affects Alice because it might be shown on Alice's profile when he leaves a comment. Impression management online and off is not just an individual act; it's a social process.

When Contexts Collide

Part of what makes impression management in a networked setting so tricky is that the contexts in which teens are operating are also networked. Contexts don't just collapse accidentally; they collapse because individuals have a different sense of where the boundaries exist and how their decisions affect others. . . .

Even when teens have a coherent sense of what they deem to be appropriate in a particular setting, their friends and peers do not necessarily share their sense of decorum and norms. Resolving the networked nature of social contexts is complicated. The "solution" that is most frequently offered is that people should not try to engage in context-dependent impression management. Indeed, Mark Zuckerberg, the founder of Facebook, is quoted as having said, "Having two identities for yourself is an example of a lack of integrity." Teens who try to manage context collapses by segregating information often suffer when that information crosses boundaries. This is particularly true when teens . . . are forced to contend with radically different social contexts that are not mutually resolvable. What makes this especially tricky for teens is that people who hold power over them often believe that they have the right to look, judge, and share, even when their interpretations may be constructed wholly out of context. . . .

Teens' Unique Struggles for Online Identities

It is important to note that the same shaming tactics that adults use to pressure teens to conform to adult standards are also used by both teens and adults to ostracize and punish youth whose identities, values, or experiences are not widely accepted. I met plenty of teens who wanted to keep secrets from their parents or teachers, but the teens who struggled the most with the challenges of collapsed contexts were those who were trying to make sense of their sexual identity or who otherwise saw themselves as outcasts in their community. Some, like Hunter—the boy from DC who was trying to navigate his "ghetto" family alongside his educationally minded friends—were simply frustrated and annoyed. Others, like teen girls who are the subject of "slut shaming" were significantly embarrassed and emotionally distraught after photos taken in the context of an intimate relationship were widely shared to shame them by using their sexuality as a weapon. Still others, like the lesbian, gay, bisexual, and transgender (LGBT) teens I met from religious and conservative backgrounds, were outright scared of what would happen if the contexts in which they were trying to operate collapsed. . . .

As teens struggle to make sense of different social contexts and present themselves appropriately, one thing becomes clear: the Internet has not evolved into an idyllic zone in which people are free from the limitations of the embodied world. Teens are struggling to make sense of who they are and how they fit into society in an environment in which contexts are networked and collapsed, audiences are invisible, and anything they say or do can easily be taken out of context. They are grappling with battles that adults face, but they are doing so while under constant surveillance and without a firm grasp of who they are. In short, they're navigating one heck of a cultural labyrinth.

FOUR

Teens Are Smart About Their Social Networking Options

Kimberly Martinez

In the following viewpoint, Kimberly Martinez, a student journalist, reviews the growing number of options for social networking online. She reports that teens are gravitating toward sites that offer community but also respect their privacy concerns. A number of newer services—particularly video-sharing platforms such as Vine, Instagram, and Snapchat—have been popular with young people, she writes. The newer platforms and utilities are simpler and more attractive than Facebook to some. According to the author, teens continue to make new technologies their own and will smartly use new tools as they become available. When this viewpoint was originally published, Kimberly Martinez was a senior at Harding High School in St. Paul, Minnesota. She is a 2013 graduate of ThreeSixty's Intermediate Journalism Camp.

Vine. Tumblr. Snapchat.

Nope, those buzzed-about terms aren't referring to the vines of a tree, tumbling in gymnastics or a quick conversation with an acquaintance. They're a few of the social media platforms vying for attention in a world dominated by Facebook and

Twitter, adding to an already long list of sites that allows teens and adults to communicate in seconds.

With more than 200 social networking sites on the Internet, the variety available has made it easier for people to craft an identity and feel a sense of connectedness.

How Teens Use Social Media

"Kids are gravitating to these other types of safe havens, wanting privacy and wanting a community," said Lisa Grimm, director of public relations and emerging media at space150, a Minneapolis-

Facebook CEO Mark Zuckerberg speaks at a media event for the launch of Instagram's video-sharing function in June 2013. Platforms that allow video sharing are particularly popular among young social media users.

based ad agency. "Being a teenager is about discovering yourself and discovering life, discovering relationships and growing and evolving and trying to figure it all out."

Katie Humphrey, a [Minneapolis, MN] *Star-Tribune* technology reporter, needs to be plugged in with new social networks so she can inform readers. It can be overwhelming for her to stay on top of evolving platforms, she said, but one trend that could be here to stay is short video sharing through Vine and Instagram.

"People I've spoken to say they like the creative outlet that some of the newer social networks offer," Humphrey said. "Facebook is still an online gathering place, but a lot of sharing and self-expression, especially among teens, is happening elsewhere through photos and video. In addition to Instagram and Vine, think Snapchat and Tumblr."

A Variety of Options Online

Released by Twitter in January, Vine boasts a maximum size of six seconds for its video. It essentially acts as an animated Twitter, with users able to post videos and add comments or captions "in the moment" as if it were real play-by-play of what's happening in front of them.

"When Twitter launched Vine, such simple video sharing was a novelty," Humphrey said.

Just a few months in, Vine now has a competitor in Video on Instagram, launched in June by Facebook, which extends video capabilities to 15 seconds. The original Instagram, with its popular photo filters, remains a major factor because of its social media novelty coupled with privacy features, which prohibit any photos you post to be saved or copied for anything else.

Then there's Tumblr, which features roughly 118 million short-form blogs where users can post text, photos, quotes, links, music and videos from a browser, phone, desktop or email.

Trent Anderson, 15, of St. Paul [Minnesota], said he uses the multi-purpose site as an archive to remember all the things he admires and is amused by. In 2013, Yahoo! bought the rights to Tumblr for $1.1 billion.

Teens' Favorite Social Networking Sites

The social networking sites most used by teens, according to a survey of 7,500 teens, average age 16.4, from 48 states.

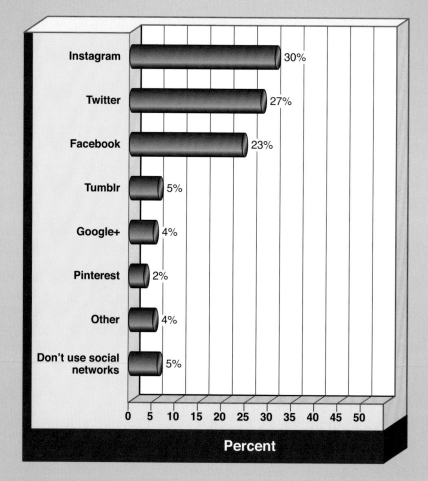

Taken from: Piper Jaffray, "27th Semi-Annual Taking Stock with Teens Survey," Spring 2014. www.piperjaffray.com.

According to the Pew Research Center's recently released "Teens, Social Media and Privacy" study, Facebook and Twitter still dominate the social media landscape, though there's room for these other platforms to make a bigger mark.

How Teens Feel About Social Media

In Pew focus groups, teens on Instagram and Twitter reported "feeling like they could better express themselves on these platforms, where they felt freed from the social expectations and constraints of Facebook." It's also predicted that "some teens may migrate their activity and attention to other sites to escape the drama and pressures they find on Facebook."

That's true of Minnesota resident Camille Ramos, 15, who uses Twitter as a way to update her thoughts without "annoying people on Facebook." Or as Samuel Dustin, 16, of St. Paul said, it's a chance to "spew your every thought into the ether."

"I think people haven't left Facebook because there's so much information there, but I also think there's so much complexity about the platform, that it can be exhausting. Now you have these different platforms that have different utility, so maybe you'll find something smaller where you don't have to share as much, and that becomes more attractive," said Amanda Lenhart, senior researcher for Pew Research Center's Internet and American Life Project in Washington, D.C.

As social media continues to evolve at a breakneck rate, Grimm said it's important for teens to do their homework and make this form of communication their own.

"Think about how these digital tools influence communication today," Grimm said. "And study what has come before so you can really apply what comes after well in order to make a bigger impact."

FIVE

Teens Say That Social Networking Makes Their Lives Better

Mary Madden et al.

The following viewpoint reports on research conducted in 2013 about teens' experiences online. Mary Madden and her colleagues write that social media and devices have become embedded in teens' daily lives and that online interactions have grown greatly in complexity. The authors found, however, that young people use a wide range of strategies to manage their privacy on social networks. Additionally, teens report that their experiences on sites such as Facebook and Twitter have been very positive. Online activities can make teens feel good about themselves and closer to others, according to the authors. Mary Madden is a researcher at the Pew Research Center. Her colleagues in this study are associated either with the Pew Research Center or the Berkman Center for Internet and Society at Harvard University.

In June 2001, the Pew Research Center's Internet & American Life Project published its first report about teenage life online and described the state of teens' experiences online this way:

Mary Madden, Amanda Lenhart, Sandra Cortesi, Urs Gasser, Maeve Duggan, Aaron Smith, and Meredith Beaton, "Teens, Social Media, and Privacy," Pew Research Internet Project, May 21, 2013. www.pewinternet.org. Copyright © 2013 Pew Research Center. All rights reserved. Reproduced by permission.

The Internet is the telephone, television, game console, and radio wrapped up in one for most teenagers and that means it has become a major "player" in many American families. Teens go online to chat with their friends, kill boredom, see the wider world, and follow the latest trends. Many enjoy doing all those things at the same time during their online sessions. Multitasking is their way of life. And the emotional hallmark of that life is enthusiasm for the new ways the Internet lets them connect with friends, expand their social networks, explore their identities, and learn new things.

This description of online life is still remarkably resonant in 2013. However, the complexity of these interactions has increased dramatically with the mass adoption of social media and mobile

Teens' Positive Experiences Online

Percent of teen Internet users who have had the following positive experiences online:

	Total teens	Sex		Age	
		Boys	Girls	12–13	14–17
	n = 778	n = 395	n = 383	n = 234	n = 544
Had experience that made you feel good about yourself	52%	51%	53%	39%	58%
Met someone online who became a good friend	39%	40%	36%	32%	42%
Had experience that made you feel closer to someone	33%	34%	32%	23%	37%

Taken from: Mary Madden et al., "Teens, Social Media, and Privacy," Pew Research Internet Project, May 21, 2013. www.pew internet.org devices. Eight in ten online teens now use social media sites. And as the Project reported earlier this year, smartphone ownership among American teens has increased substantially; half of teen smartphone owners now say they *mostly* go online using their phone.

While social media and the devices that connect teens and their families have become increasingly valuable and deeply embedded into daily life, the concurrent rise in the economic value of the social media platforms and the advertising models that support them have raised concerns among policymakers and privacy advocates. As we reported in our "Parents, Teens and Online Privacy" report late last year, the policy community is wrestling with the new reality of the enormous amount of information that is shared by children and adults in digital environments and the ways that information can be collected, shared and sold as new form of digital currency. . . .

This [viewpoint] covers findings from a nationally representative survey of U.S. teens ages 12–17 and their parents, interspersed with focus group findings from online focus groups conducted before the national survey, and in-person focus groups conducted by the Berkman Center this spring.

Teens and Privacy Concerns

What emerges is a portrait of teens who engage in a range of behaviors to manage the boundaries of their "social privacy" online. Far from being privacy indifferent, these youth are mindful about what they post, even if their primary focus and motivation is often their engagement with an audience of peers and family, rather than how their online behavior might be tracked by advertisers or other third parties.

While some do report concerns about third-party access to their social media postings, and some say they encounter advertising online that is inappropriate for their age, privacy from businesses and advertisers is not top of mind for most teens. However, this generally echoes other studies of concern among adults, which suggest that there is a persistent minority of the public that expresses strong

Social networking can help build friendships. Four in ten teens say they have met a good friend online.

concerns about institutional and commercial access to personal information. In contrast, parent concern levels with regard to their children are relatively high overall, a finding that has been documented in other recent studies of parents with teenage children.

Patterns of teen social media use change with age, and this has important implications for understanding the evolution of teens' personal privacy strategies. Younger teens, who are often newer users to social media platforms, tend to have smaller networks and do not post as much content to their profiles. Older teens, who are more frequent users of social media sites, have amassed larger networks and tend to be friends with a wider range of people on sites like Facebook. . . .

In the current survey, we wanted to understand the broader context of teens' online lives beyond Facebook and Twitter and the context in which teens wrestled with all the privacy options before them. And while many teens report positive experiences online, such as making friends and feeling closer to another person, some encounter unwanted content and contact from others.

Positive Experiences for Teens

Half of online teens say they have had an experience online that made them feel good about themselves.

Looking at some of the experiences teens have online, many report positive outcomes. In a broad question about all online activity that was asked of all teen Internet users, 52% of online teens said they had an experience *online* that made them feel good about themselves. Among teen social media users, 57% said they had an experience online that made them feel good, compared with just 30% of teen Internet users who do not use social media. In keeping with the age-related findings we reported in 2011, older teens are much more likely to report a positive experience of this kind; 58% of those ages 14–17 said this compared with 39% of those ages 12–13. Girls and boys are equally as likely to report feel-good experiences, and quite strikingly, these positive experiences are universally felt across all socioeconomic groups. However, youth living in urban areas (44%) are less likely than those living in suburban (55%) and rural (61%) areas to say that they have had an experience online that made them feel good about themselves.

One in three online teens say they have had an experience online that made them feel closer to another person.

Many online teens also say they have had online experiences that made them feel closer to someone else; in our current survey, 33% of all online teens reported a deepened connection to someone because of something that happened online. Looking at teen social media users, 37% report having an experience somewhere online that made them feel closer to another person, compared with just 16% of online teens who do not use social media. In a similar question asked in 2011, 58% of social media–using teens said they had an experience *on a social network site* that made them feel closer to someone else.

Again, a teen's age is closely associated with this kind of positive outcome from online experience. While 37% of online teens ages 14–17 reported having an experience online that made them feel closer to another person, just 23% of online teens ages 12–13 said they had this experience. Girls and boys are equally as likely to report online experiences that made them feel closer to someone else, and once again, there were no notable differences across socioeconomic groups.

Online teens living in urban areas are less likely than those living in suburban areas to say they had an online experience that made them feel closer to another person (28% vs. 39%).

39% of online teens say they have met someone online who became a good friend.

Four in ten online teens say they have met someone online who later became a good friend. African-American teens are more likely than white teens to report meeting good friends online; 54% of African-American teen Internet users say they have met a good friend online compared with 35% of white teens. Boys and girls are equally likely to report meeting good friends online, but older online teens ages 14–17 are more likely than younger teens to say they have met a close friend online (42% vs. 32%). Teens living in the lowest-income households (earning less than $30,000 per year) are more likely than those living in the higher-income households (earning $50,000 or more per year) to say that they have met a good friend online (53% vs. 30%). Internet-using teens living in rural areas are more likely than those living in suburban areas to say that they have met a good friend online (50% vs. 36%).

SIX

Social Networking Can Be an Important Educational Tool

Barbara Christiansen

Although some teens may have difficulty imagining their teachers using social media, educators can use social media sites as tools in the classroom, Barbara Christiansen explains in the following viewpoint. One reason many teachers do not use social media in the classroom is a lack of training, the author reports. Another important challenge is managing the online boundaries between a teacher's personal and professional lives. Christiansen also reports on teachers who have found a balance between the two and are sharing their success stories with other educators. Social networking is proving helpful in the classroom as well as in school administration and professional development, the author writes. Barbara Christiansen is a reporter for the *Daily Herald* newspaper in Provo, Utah.

Most teenagers and even younger children seem to be social media experts. They communicate multiple times a day, often multiple times an hour.

But what about the adults in their lives? Say, their teachers?

Many would find it difficult to imagine their teachers tweeting or posting a selfie. And many of their teachers can't imagine it either, but for different reasons.

However, there are some teachers who use social media, not only with their friends, but with their students.

A national survey by the University of Phoenix showed that 80 percent of teachers worry about using social media with students and their parents.

Main Reasons Teachers Do Not Use Social Media

"There are two big reasons why they worry," said John Shoell, college campus chair for the College of Education at the University of Phoenix Utah campus. "Sixty-nine percent of those surveyed felt that parents might sometimes use social media networks to monitor teachers' social lives. The second is a lack of training."

The survey showed that fewer than one-third of the teachers have had training on how to use social media to connect with their students or as an educational tool.

"It has been evolving," he said. "It is a tool that the education community needs to embrace and gain ways to help the teachers in the field know how to use social media to enhance their classrooms."

There are many who aren't ready for that connection, however.

Issues Faced by Education Professionals

More than a third of those who do use it have had issues with students or parents attempting to connect with them. Perhaps that is why only 17 percent encouraged their students to connect with them.

"Many professionals face challenges navigating how and when to use social media and whether they should merge their personal and professional lives," said Kathy Cook, director of educational technology for the University of Phoenix College of Education. "Perhaps nowhere is the line more blurred than for teachers. On one hand, social media can be a valuable tool for learning and

"And if you can't make it to class, at least follow me on Twitter."

"Ornithology teacher: 'And if you can't make it to class, at least follow me on Twitter,'" cartoon by Jonny Hawkins, www.CartoonStock.com. Copyright © Jonny Hawkins. Reproduction rights obtainable from www.CartoonStock.com.

connecting with students and parents; on the other, it can invite inappropriate behavior and misuse."

Incorporating Social Media in the Classroom

Daniel Potter of Westlake High School [in Saratoga Springs, Utah] is one who has found that balancing point. He started as an intern at Westlake five years ago.

"I noticed a small amount of students never parting with their phones," he said. "I played the police patrol and told them to put them away. I didn't want to see it. But I knew that phones were part of their day-to-day routines."

Now Westlake has an open technology policy, he said.

"Phones are not going away," he said. "The school encouraged us to find ways to incorporate the phones."

Potter teaches English 11, technical writing and mythology. He has encouraged his students to learn to condense their writing into the equivalent of a tweet. He said the students are usually good at gathering information and passing it on, but they were not as experienced in creating information. They are working together to overcome that.

"It has been a pretty good partnership," he said. "I had never heard of Twitter, but I saw enough students sneaking, using Twitter on their phones. I started collaborating with them and tried it out."

That brought about a difference in how the students used social media.

"When they first came into the classroom, their messages were egocentric and about mundane things," he said. "We talked about how we could make things more relevant. It has been fun."

Sharing Success Stories with Other Teachers

The word has gotten around and when students enter his classroom for the first time, they inquire if he is the teacher who lets them keep their phones. When he confirms that he is, they seem relieved.

"We don't need to go back to the archaic and tell them to put their phones away," he said. "I am not trying to take it away, but to expand their repertoire. The end goal is for them to be better writers, better readers."

Potter is careful how he uses social media with the students.

"I haven't really had any worries," he said. "Knowing the purpose, this won't be a place for me to post pictures of my family."

He has expanded his use of social media to reach other educators.

"It is like an online teacher's lounge," he said. "We talk about ideas, lesson plans, anything I want to bring into my classroom."

Some teachers allow students to keep their cell phones in the classroom and use the opportunity to incorporate social media into the curriculum.

He has received most of his training from the students and others on a practical basis.

"I personally haven't had any formal training," he said. "I would recommend the district show us best practices and that we have conversations between faculty members."

Cody Spendlove, educational technology director for Alpine School District [Utah], said the district was moving toward similar goals.

"There has been a major shift at the professional development center at the district office," he said. "It is something we are working on."

Other School Uses for Social Networking

Shoell gave some examples of professional use of social media.

"It can be used to disseminate information about the school —calendar events, reminders for parents, important things coming up, clubs might post pictures," he said. "It is a great tool for sharing of information."

At the University of Phoenix, it goes to another level. Called Phoenix Connect, it includes opportunities for students to communicate with each other and with faculty members.

"We use it as a professional development tool to collaborate with faculty," Shoell said. "Some of them are spread out along the Wasatch Front. It can help share information, best practices, collaborate on coursework."

He said schools should take time to address the rules.

"Every school has an opportunity at the beginning of the school year," he said. "There are open houses or back to school nights where there are opportunities to meet with the parents. That would be an ideal time to indicate—this is the method of communication I would like to use throughout the year. You are setting boundaries and being very consistent."

Benefits of Social Media Use in Schools

He has seen two benefits to using social media.

"It can be used very effectively as a tool for the dissemination of important information," he said. "Social media tools would be a great source for that sharing on information that is pertinent to the school and students' success."

"Second is professional development and the opportunities for teachers to collaborate with each other," he said. "There is a wealth of technical resources that are available and education specific that give us the opportunity to collaborate and share ideas and help strengthen each other."

SEVEN

Social Networking Exposes Teens to Dating Violence

Janine M. Zweig, Meredith Dank, Pamela Lachman, and Jennifer Yahner

The authors of the following viewpoint report on a study by the National Institute of Justice that examined the use of technology in teen dating violence and abuse. The study greatly expands current knowledge about cyberdating abuse and cyberbullying. It concludes that rates of online abuse are substantial and usually combined with other forms of abuse. The authors also explain that while girls are vulnerable to online abuse, they are also perpetrators and that youth with alternative sexual identities are particularly vulnerable. Janine M. Zweig is a senior fellow and Meredith Dank, Pamela Lachman, and Jennifer Yahner are research associates at the Justice Policy Center of the Urban Institute in Washington, DC.

In 2011, the National Institute of Justice funded the Urban Institute's Justice Policy Center to examine the role of youth technology use in teen dating violence and abuse and bullying. The goal of the project was to expand knowledge about the types of violence and abuse experiences youth have, the extent of victimization and perpetration via technology and new media (e.g., social networking sites, texting on cell phones), and how the experience of such cyber abuse within teen dating relationships or through bullying relates to other life factors. . . .

Study Findings on Teen Dating Violence and Abuse

- More than a quarter (26 percent) of youth in a relationship and nearly a fifth (18 percent) of all youth said they experienced some form of cyber dating abuse victimization in the prior year. Youth experienced cyber dating abuse at a rate that was comparable to that of physical dating violence, about half that of psychological dating abuse, and twice that of sexual coercion.
- Females were twice as likely as males to report being a victim of sexual cyber dating abuse and/or sexual coercion in the prior year. Male youth, on the other hand, reported significantly higher rates of all forms of physical dating violence victimization.
- Few victims of any teen dating violence or abuse sought help after such experiences. Less than one out of ten victims reported seeking help, with half as many male victims as female victims seeking help.
- More than a tenth (12 percent) of youth in a relationship and nearly a tenth (8 percent) of all youth said they had perpetrated cyber dating abuse in the prior year. Youth reports of cyber dating abuse perpetration were about half that of physical dating violence and/or psychological dating abuse perpetration, yet four times that of self-reported sexual coercion perpetration.
- Females reported greater levels of non-sexual cyber dating abuse perpetration than males. By contrast, male youth were significantly more likely to report perpetrating sexual cyber dating abuse.
- Lesbian, gay, bisexual, transgender, and questioning (LGBTQ) youth reported significantly higher rates of cyber dating abuse victimization and perpetration than heterosexual youth. Thirty-seven percent of LGBTQ youth reported

Teen girls are far more likely than boys to report being victims of cyberbullying, and the majority of victims do not seek help.

cyber dating abuse victimization and about half that reported perpetrating such violence.

- Cyber dating abuse had the greatest degree of overlap with psychological dating abuse; 84 percent of cyber dating abuse victims also reported psychological dating abuse victimizations, and 73 percent of cyber dating abuse perpetrators also reported psychological dating abuse perpetration. Among cyber dating abuse victims, 52 percent also reported physical dating violence victimization and 33 percent reported sexual coercion victimization. Among cyber dating abuse perpetrators, 55 percent also reported physical dating violence perpetration and 11 percent reported sexual coercion perpetration.

- Cyber dating abuse victims and perpetrators were more than two and three times as likely, respectively, as non-victims and non-perpetrators to also report experiencing and/or perpetrating cyber bullying behaviors against non-intimates.

- The life factors that had the strongest overall correlations to cyber dating abuse victimization, when other factors were statistically controlled (e.g., age, race, school socioeconomic status [SES]), included being female, having committed a higher number of delinquent behaviors, previous engagement in sexual activity, reporting a higher level of recent depression, and reporting a higher level of recent anger/hostility.
- The life factors that had the strongest overall correlations to cyber dating abuse perpetration, when other life factors were statistically controlled, included being female, spending a higher number of hours per day on the cell phone, more frequent alcohol and/or serious drug use, having committed a higher number of delinquent behaviors, previously having engaged in sexual activity, reporting a higher level of recent depression, reporting a higher level of recent anger/hostility, and engaging in fewer prosocial activities. . . .

Study Findings on Bullying

- One in six youth (17 percent) reported being victims of cyber bullying in the past year and more than twice that share reported being victims of physical and/or psychological bullying.
- Female youth reported significantly higher victimization rates with regard to cyber bullying and psychological bullying; in particular, girls were twice as likely as boys to report being a victim of cyber bullying in the prior year. By contrast, male youth reported significantly higher rates of physical bullying victimization.
- One out of six bullying victims reported seeking help, with twice as many female victims as male victims seeking help.
- Fewer than one in ten youth reported perpetrating cyber bullying in the prior year, while a quarter to a third of youth said they had perpetrated physical bullying and/or psychological bullying during that time. Slightly less than half of the youth

Cyber Dating Abuse Among Male and Female Youth

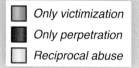
- Only victimization
- Only perpetration
- Reciprocal abuse

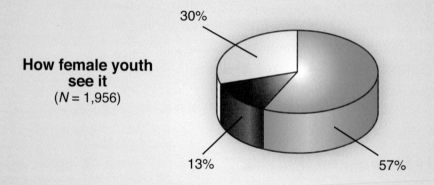

How female youth see it
(*N* = 1,956)

30%

13%

57%

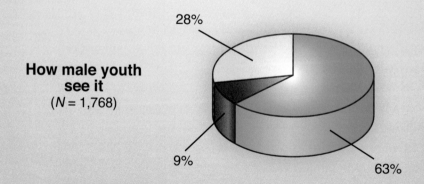

How male youth see it
(*N* = 1,768)

28%

9%

63%

Taken from: Janine M. Zweig et al. "Technology, Teen Dating Violence and Abuse, and Bullying," Urban Institute, July 2013. www.urban.org.

who reported cyber bullying victimization also claimed that they perpetrated cyber bullying.

- Female youth reported significantly higher perpetration rates with regard to cyber bullying, while male youth reported significantly higher rates of physical bullying perpetration.
- LGBTQ youth reported significantly higher rates of cyber bullying victimization and perpetration than heterosexual youth. One-quarter of LGBTQ youth reported being a victim of cyber bullying and half that report perpetrating such violence.
- Nine out of ten cyber bullying victims also experienced psychological bullying victimization, and the same portion of cyber bullying perpetrators also perpetrated psychological bullying. There was also a fairly high degree of overlap between cyber bullying and physical bullying, with two-thirds to three-quarters of cyber bullying victims/perpetrators also reporting physical bullying victimization/perpetration.
- Cyber bullying victims and perpetrators were almost three and four times as likely, respectively, as non-victims and non-perpetrators to also report experiencing and/or perpetrating cyber dating abuse against romantic partners.
- The life factors that had the strongest overall correlations to cyber bullying victimization, when other life factors were statistically controlled (e.g., age, race, school SES) included being female, white, of younger age, spending more hours per day on the cell phone, being less emotionally close to one's parents while having more frequent communication with parents (not necessarily of a positive nature), more frequent alcohol use, having previously engaged in sexual activity, reporting a higher level of recent depression, and reporting a higher level of recent anger/hostility.
- The life factors that had the strongest overall correlations to cyber bullying perpetration, when other life factors were statistically controlled (e.g., age, race, school SES) included being female, of younger age, being less emotionally close to one's parents yet having more frequent communication with parents (not necessarily of a positive nature), more frequent

alcohol use, having committed a higher number of delinquent behaviors previously, having previously engaged in sexual activity, and reporting a higher level of recent anger/hostility.

Seven Conclusions Drawn from the Studies

Based on the above findings, we draw seven general conclusions related to cyber dating abuse and cyber bullying:

1. Rates of cyber abuse are substantial.
2. Cyber abuse is often combined with other forms of dating violence and abuse or other forms of bullying. Further, cyber dating abuse and cyber bullying experiences also overlap, for both victims and perpetrators.
3. Despite this overlap between cyber abuse and other forms of violence and abuse or bullying, some youth *only* experience cyber abuse, making it and its correlates important to distinguish.
4. Most cyber abuse victims do not perpetrate cyber abuse, but most perpetrators also report victimization.
5. Females are particularly vulnerable to cyber abuse, but are also perpetrators of cyber abuse.
6. LGBTQ youth are particularly vulnerable to all types of teen dating violence/abuse and bullying, including cyber dating abuse and cyber bullying.
7. Few victims of teen dating violence and abuse and/or bullying seek help.

EIGHT

Social Networking Can Help Prevent Sexual Assault

Ann Friedman

> The following viewpoint was originally published shortly after the conclusion of the Steubenville, Ohio, rape trial in 2013. The victim in that case had been victimized further by the unauthorized dissemination on social media of images of her after the assault. According to the viewpoint author, however, social media can also empower victims of sexual assault and can be used to identify and apprehend perpetrators. Viewpoint author Ann Friedman argues that technology is not to blame for the victimization of women online. Despite the dangers women face online, they can be the drivers of technology, and social networking can play a role in women's empowerment and protection by helping prevent sexual assault. Ann Friedman is a journalist and a regular columnist for *New York* magazine on politics, culture, and gender.

Earlier this week [March 2013], on the heels of guilty verdicts in the Steubenville [Ohio] case of two [Steubenville High School] football players who sexually assaulted a girl and broadcast it on social media, teenagers in the town of Torrington, Connecticut, were blowing up Facebook and Twitter with vile,

Sexual Solicitations of Youth Online Are Decreasing

Percent of teens who say they have received unwanted sexual solicitations online:

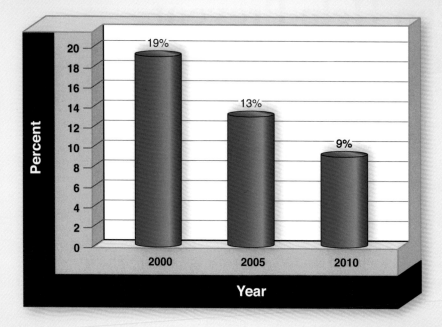

Note: Unwanted sexual solicitations include unwelcome requests to engage in sexual activities or sexual talk, or to give personal sexual information, whether or not made by an adult.

Taken from: Kimberly J. Mitchell et al., "Trends in Unwanted Sexual Solicitations: Findings from the Youth Internet Safety Studies," Crimes Against Children Research Center, February 2014. www.unh.edu/ccrc.

victim-blaming comments about a 13-year-old who says she was raped by two 18-year-old football players. If we hadn't been aware before, this week has made clear that, in the digital era, the accuser and the accused are not the only parties involved in sexual assault cases. We're all bystanders on social networks.

Social media has been rightly hailed for bringing the Steubenville crime to light. Texts, tweets, and photos were essential to establishing that this was not a consensual act and not a "he said/she said" story. Yet paradoxically, both the Steubenville and Torrington rape cases have escalated the narrative—one that's swirled around ever since the days of A/S/L [age/sex/location] queries in AOL chatrooms—that the Internet is jeopardizing the privacy and safety of teens. And, in particular, teen girls.

Before it was even available in every home, let alone every purse and pocket in America, adults were worried that the Internet would enable sexual assault and stalking of naïve teens, who would log on and reveal details about themselves to older predators. As we welcomed Web 2.0 and smartphones and broadband into our lives, it became clear that their peers perhaps posed a greater risk, as social media became the place where bullying and rumor-mongering—practices as old as schoolyard itself—became easy to spread at the click of a button. The case of Amanda Todd took these fears to a horrifying extreme: The Canadian teenager was so brutally harassed after a topless photo of her made the rounds in her high school that she eventually committed suicide.

Social Networking and Rape Victims

Even though the Steubenville case involved the malicious spread of information online—photos of the passed-out victim were plastered all over social media without her consent—the fact that the case ended in two rape convictions notably revealed that social media is not always negative for young women. "Cellphone videos can be forwarded to authorities, not circulated as jokes," writes Amanda Hess at *Slate*. "Text messages can be used to identify rapists, not shame victims. And photos can establish central facts, not publicize humiliation."

When issuing the Steubenville verdict, Judge Thomas Lipps warned teens to think about "how you record things on the social media so prevalent today." Lipps, with his finger-wagging tone, is not alone in his fears about the effects of Instagram and Twitter and Facebook. As columnist Kathleen Parker writes this week in the *Washington Post*, "What hasn't been addressed is the factor of social media in the events themselves." She wonders whether our tendency to 'gram and tweet the tiniest details has detached us from events unfolding in front of our faces, some modern form of the psychological effect that murder victim Kitty Genovese[1] ushered in almost 60 years ago. The implication is that all of the high schoolers who tweeted and retweeted and texted the violence that was perpetrated against this girl in Ohio would have somehow been more likely to intervene in a pre-digital era. Decades of research on the Bystander Effect[2] has shown us that's not true, which means the Internet is once again acquitted. Bullies, killers, and rapists are the problem, not the medium by which they broadcast their crimes.

The Internet and Women's Empowerment

In almost every prominent news story about how the dynamics of social media play out offline, young women are set up as victims

The Steubenville High School football stadium is seen in the town of Steubenville, Ohio, where two students were found guilty of raping a classmate after posting the incident on social media.

rather than agents and drivers of technology. The case has been made repeatedly that the digital era puts young women at risk in new ways—they can be stalked with smartphones, slut-shamed on instant messenger, targeted by rapists on social media. But the Internet can also be a source of power and protection—and I'm not just talking about accountability in rape cases. (A [2013] report by the Pew Internet and American Life Project finds that 34 percent of teen girls "mostly go online using their cell phone," compared with 24 percent of teen boys. "This is notable since boys and girls are equally likely to be smartphone owners," the study says.) I use an app called CheckOn.Me, which notifies a select group of contacts if I fail to log in to the app after, say, meeting up with some unknown Craigslist seller about buying a chair. More generally, social media allows me a way to casually check up on friends. If I know a friend of mine was on a blind date the night before, I confess that I am slightly relieved when I see a new tweet from her in the morning or that she's liked something on Facebook. For all the headlines about women being creeped online, it's easy to forget that, far more often, social media provides new ways to blow the whistle.

The Internet isn't some lawless netherworld, it's merely a reflection of social dynamics—and yes, sometimes crimes—that occur in the offline world. Put another way, by Sarah Gram in an essay about teen girls and selfies, "Do we honestly think that by ceasing to take and post selfies, the bodies of young women would cease to be spectacles?" If we didn't have Instagram pictures and tweets about it, the rape that occurred in Steubenville wouldn't be any less real. It just would have been less documented. I agree with Judge Lipps that we should all think about how we're using social media: Rather than just recognizing its potential to hurt and expose, start appreciating how it enables us to help keep each other safe.

Notes

1. In a widely publicized 1964 case, Catherine "Kitty" Genovese was murdered at the entrance to her Queens, New York,

apartment building. Neighbors and bystanders failed to intervene or to contact the police despite hearing the attack and her calls for help.

2. "The term *bystander effect* refers to the phenomenon in which the greater the number of people present, the less likely people are to help a person in distress. When an emergency situation occurs, observers are more likely to take action if there are few or no other witnesses." (Kendra Cherry, "The Bystander Effect," About.com. http://psychology.about.com /od/socialpsychology/a/bystandereffect.htm)

NINE

Social Networking Exposes Girls to Sexual Abuse

Laura Bates

> In the following viewpoint, a British writer reports on the
> spread of so-called question-and-answer websites. The sites
> are popular with young girls, who are then subjected to
> sexually explicit messages and requests from anonymous
> users, according to the author. The viewpoint recounts
> stories of young girls who received abusive and sexually
> explicit messages on sites such as ask.fm, formspring.me,
> and qooh.me. The author writes that the messages reflect
> a larger problem in society with sexism and that zero
> tolerance for violence and abuse in relationships should
> be taught in schools. Laura Bates is the founder of the
> Everyday Sexism Project, a collection of women's daily
> experiences of gender inequality. She has written for *The
> Independent*, the *Huffington Post*, *Grazia*, the Women's
> Media Center, and *JUMP!* magazine for girls.

A new breed of social media websites is leaving young people
open to cyber bullying, with anonymous users able to bombard others with sexually explicit messages and demands.

Despite little mainstream media coverage, "question and
answer" websites such as ask.fm, qooh.me and formspring.me

have exploded in popularity. More than 29 million Formspring accounts have been created since its 2009 launch.

The sites allow users to sign up for a profile, with a name and photograph. Others can then ask questions completely anonymously, some open to all, some directed to a specific profile. Users choose which questions to answer, with the option to "like" answers, and in some cases, to share them on well known sites such

Anonymous question-and-answer websites such as ask.fm can expose young girls to sexual pressure and bullying.

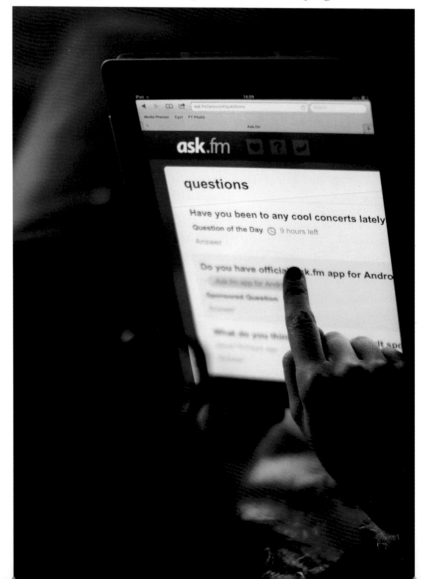

as Facebook and Twitter. The anonymity provided by the sites has made them a hotbed for sexual pressure, bullying and abuse.

A Torrent of Disturbing Posts

Browsing some of the sites for just a few minutes reveals a torrent of sexual demands, explicit questions and abusive threats to users whose photos suggest they are young teenage girls. Posts included: "You're a fat, ugly, worthless piece of s***. Please kill yourself," "Can we have sex?" and "Wanna do it dirty?"

One mother, aged 32, asked her 13-year-old daughter's permission to let *The Independent* view her ask.fm profile, where other users, many claiming to be from her school, had posted a string of aggressively sexual questions: "Have you ever sucked a d***?"; "Do you shave your pubes?"; "Bra size?"; "Can I bang you?"

They call her "slut", make sexual demands and threats and in one case, ask her to upload a video of "you cutting yourself". The mother said: "Even in year five at a Catholic primary school, the emails she used to receive from the lads in her year were obscene and disturbing." Her daughter was later diagnosed with anorexia and depression, took an overdose and spent 11 weeks in a mental health unit.

Elizabeth Muncey, a 27-year-old actor from London, contacted *The Independent* in shock after reading her 13-year-old sister's text messages and Facebook page. She says: "I couldn't believe the frequency with which she and her friends were being referred to as 'sluts', 'whores' and 'slags'. The boys in her peer group also seemed to be behaving in aggressive and manipulative ways, coercing them to do things they didn't want to."

If they bowed to the pressure, they were then "shamed" for it. On the ask.fm site, her sister received countless abusive messages such as: "You dirty little year eight" [eighth grader] and "whore".

Turning Abuse into a Joke

Many entries to the Everyday Sexism Project, which catalogues instances of sexism experienced by women on a day-to-day basis,

Most Popular "Trolling" Sites

The most popular sites and services for online trolling or bullying, according to the Knowthenet survey

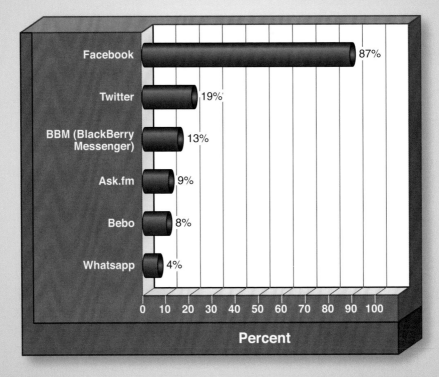

Taken from: Damien Gayle, "Facebook Is the Worst Social Network for Bullying with 19-Year-Old Boys the Most Common Victims," *Daily Mail* (UK), March 15, 2013. www.dailymail.co.uk.

refer to incidents of young people joking about rape and sexual violence without technology coming into play at all, such as the year 11 boy, aged 15 or 16, reported to have said "rape is a compliment really" in a classroom discussion. Nick Batley, 22, a volunteer sex educator with Sexpression, said this lack of understanding about consent and sexual violence is common among young people, both on and offline. While working with pupils aged 11 to 15, one told him: "Girls have a reputation to uphold . . . boys are meant to break that."

Both Formspring and ask.fm did not respond to requests for comment. Vince Mabuza, the founder of qooh.me, said: "Cyber bullying is a huge problem on sites like qooh.me and the others. I have sleepless nights trying to come up with solutions to stop this. [But] shutting the site down won't help, because new ones will be created and the cycle will repeat itself. What we have done is to give users some control by allowing them to disable the anonymous part of the site."

Today, as part of the global One Billion Rising campaign to end violence against women and girls, the [British] government will debate making "personal, social and health education, including a zero tolerance approach to violence and abuse in relationships, a requirement in schools."

TEN

Social Networking Helps the LGBT Rights Movement

Esther Glasionov, Rita Hage, Luke Stevenson, and Madeline Tallman

The following viewpoint considers how lesbian, gay, bisexual, and transgendered (LGBT) communities in three different countries—the United States, Russia, and Egypt—have used social networking. The authors write that LGBT communities have historically suffered from political and economic discrimination. Social media is being used, however, to disseminate information about formerly marginalized groups and to give voice to their viewpoints. The authors give specific examples of how social media has been used to promote and support LGBT issues and rights in these three very different countries. When they authored this report in 2013, Esther Glasionov, Rita Hage, Luke Stevenson, and Madeline Tallman were students at the Salzburg Academy on Media and Global Change in Austria.

The history of LGBT communities is laced with hardship over their political and economic rights under the law, their social acceptance and their personal safety. Members of these diverse

Esther Glasionov, Rita Hage, Luke Stevenson, and Madeline Tallman, "Social Media and the LGBT Community," Salzburg Academy on Media and Global Change, International Center for Media and the Public Agenda, 2013. www.salzburg.umd.edu . Copyright © 2013 Salzburg Global Seminar. Reproduced by permission.

communities have suffered discrimination, violence, and a denial of their very identity.

In the past decade, countries around the world have seen tremendous growth in support for people who identify as LGBT (or other sexual orientations and identities that differ from heterosexuality). At the same time, there has also been a huge growth of Internet and social media use.

This [viewpoint] focuses on how social media have been used as a resource by LGBT communities and their allies as a way to rally and gain support and rights for their members in ways that were impossible before the Internet.

Social Networking and the US LGBT Community

In the United States, LGBT rights have expanded rapidly with the recent legalization of same-sex marriage in 13 states and the District of Columbia. With the surge of support for LGBT rights, (as of 2013 roughly between 49 and 58 percent of the U.S. population supports same-sex marriage) there has been a surge in LGBT social media campaigns.

The It Gets Better Project was one of the first social media campaigns that successfully reached out to teens—both gay and straight. The 2010 campaign started after Justin Aaberg and Billy Lucas, two American teenage boys, committed suicide after intense bullying for being gay. Dan Savage, a sexual health columnist, and his partner Terry Miller used YouTube to post an eight-minute video describing Savage's own struggles as a gay man and how he overcame harassment and unacceptance. He was joined by young and old gay, lesbian, bisexual, transgendered and allied supporters, speaking out about their own experiences and how their lives as adults "got better"—even with their hardships. Within months, dozens of other celebrities created their own videos calling for support of LGBT teens and the end of bullying. Within three years the project has gathered more than 50,000 user-created videos in support of LGBT teens, including videos from President Barack Obama and former Secretary of State Hillary Clinton.

Online Behaviors of LGBT Adults in the United States

Percentage of all lesbian, gay, bisexual, and transgender (LGBT) adults who:

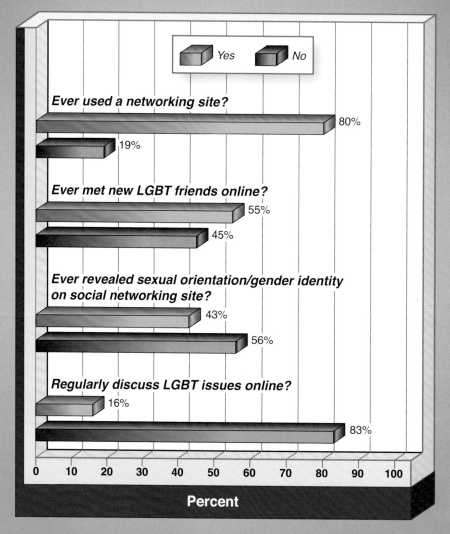

Taken from: Pew Research Center, "A Survey of LGBT Americans: Attitudes, Experiences and Values in Changing Times," June 13, 2013. www.pewsocialtrends.org

LGBT activists in the United States have also used Twitter to gain supporters. Activists' remarkable success at reaching out to a broad community via Twitter has suggested that social media may be more effective in raising awareness, especially among youth, than traditional media. In 2013 U.S. President Barack Obama tweeted his support of same-sex marriage shortly after the Supreme Court overruled the Defense of Marriage Act (DOMA), a federal law that would have allowed states to deny marriage and the financial benefits of marriage to same-sex couples. Obama's short tweet reached 150 million people—a number that dwarfs the audience of newspapers, broadcast television and radio.

Other social media campaigns by US-based LGBT activists to raise awareness for the cause, include an initiative started by the Human Rights Campaign (HRC) which encouraged marriage equality supporters to change their Facebook profile picture to the HRC "equality" logo. . . .

Russian Oppression Addressed by Online Activists

In Russia, LGBT activists have faced greater challenges to using social media on behalf of LGBT rights in part due to legislation. On June 30, 2013, for example, the lower house of parliament passed a measure into law that "ban[ned] the promotion of homosexual propaganda and mandate[d] stiff fines and jail terms for violators." The law in effect made it illegal to equate straight and gay relationships, as well as to distribute material on gay rights.

As a consequence, in July 2013, a group of four Dutch tourists who were working on a documentary in Russia about gay rights were arrested for "promoting homosexual relations among minors" and subsequently were banned from entering Russia for three years.

Also in July 2013, prominent Russian gay activist, Nikolai Alexeyev, who created an online petition with an intent to blacklist visas for Yelena Mizulina and Vitaly Milonov—two Russian lawmakers who he said were responsible for the federal law—was in turn, threatened with a criminal case by the two lawmakers.

Because Russia is limiting people's voices with its new legislation, Russians and others from all over the world took to social media to protest this law and stand up for the LGBT community.

Dan Savage, founder of It Gets Better, called on his blog for a boycott of Russian vodka in response to the law. Savage picked out the popular Stolichnaya and Russian Standard brands and used the hashtag #dumpStoli to popularize the campaign. The campaign was also backed by Queer Nation, an LGBT American activist group, as well as the Russian-American gay rights group Rusa LGBT.

In response to the #dumpStoli campaign, bars in the United States, Canada, Great Britain, and Australia stopped serving the two brands. Following all of this, Stolichnaya's Latvia-based manufacturer, the SPI Group and founder Val Mendeleev, posted an open letter condemning "the dreadful actions taken by the Russian Government" and stating that Stolichnaya "has always been, and continues to be a fervent supporter and friend to the LGBT community."

Even celebrities, such as Lady Gaga, who is a prominent supporter of equal rights, has taken to raising her voice where she posted support on Facebook to Russians.

The Egyptian Twitter Revolution and the LGBT Community

Ten years before the "Arab Spring," on May 11, 2001, Egyptian police raided a gay nightclub on the Queen Boat in Cairo and arrested 52 homosexuals, then tortured and raped some of those in detention. Twenty-three of those arrested "were convicted for debauchery and defaming Islam and sentenced up to five years in prison with hard labour." The national media published the names, photos and professions of those arrested, in a bid to publically humiliate them and their families.

Ten years later a new Egypt emerged in Tahrir Square, Cairo, which took down President Hosni Mubarak. But even after the ouster of Mubarak, LGBT activists struggled for their rights; the LGBT community's bid for recognition did not meet with

Dan Savage (left) and his husband, Terry Miller, wear shirts to promote the It Gets Better Project at New York City's LGBT Pride March in 2011.

universal acceptance: "Riding the revolutionary wave after the ouster of Mubarak, some gay activists called for an LGBT stand on Tahrir . . . but were quickly silenced by others in the community" [according to journalist Bel Trew].

That prompted rethinking. Twitter and Facebook did not cause the Arab revolutions, but were used as powerful tools to communicate breaking events and to organize and schedule protests and demonstrations. So LGBT activists also turned to social media. Ramy Youssef, a young gay Egyptian, used Twitter to enlist support for other LGBT Egyptians. Youssef, 21, came out about his sexuality through Twitter and was consequently shunned by his family, and beaten up and robbed by others in his community. Then through his anti-homophobia campaign on Twitter, he attempted to "bring a community together." His tweets quickly went viral and "within hours [they] had drawn thousands of retweets and mentions, quickly gaining support from mainstream activists and celebrities." Youssef also mounted Facebook events to emphasize and bring up issues of homophobia, while also making others aware of the unacceptable homophobic language used in the country.

Youssef is one example of how social media can help narrate events, share news and create a public forum. Global Voices, an international network of bloggers and citizen journalists, for example, reported on how the Twitter hashtag that Youssef used had created a space for dialogue between both Egyptian supporters and opponents of LGBT rights. . . .

LGBT activists had found an online place to raise their voices and create larger campaigns for acceptance and recognition. In 2013, for example, "in honor of the Queen Boat incident, gay rights activists in Egypt decided to mark May 11 as the 'Egyptian Day Against Homophobia' (EDAHO)" [as reported by news website Aswat Masriya English]. That week, activists launched online campaigns to get supporters to tweet and blog for LGBT rights. That same year pro-LGBT activists transformed "an anti-gay mural on Mohamed Mahmoud Street in Cairo, which took a swing at the city's cops calling them gay." Activists altered the homophobic graffiti to promote a pro-gay message. . . .

Addressing Civil Rights with Social Media

Youths and political activists around the world have been early adopters of social media, recognizing the personal and professional opportunities that platforms such as Twitter and Facebook have offered. Civil rights movements have followed in their wake, noting that social media excels at exactly what they need to do: identify, educate and mobilize diverse groups. The global LGBT community has used Facebook, Twitter, YouTube and other platforms to shape people's attitudes towards LGBT issues. Via social media, LGBT groups have offered support to members of the community, and have gathered together the critical mass of voices that is needed to effect change, such as the legalization of gay marriage in the United States. In countries where LGBT members have been under attack, such as in Russia and Egypt, social media has taken on an advocacy role, hoping via greater transparency to ameliorate repression and ultimately build local support for LGBT issues.

ELEVEN

Social Networking Enables Real Political Change

Yousri Marzouki and Olivier Oullier

In the following viewpoint, two behavioral scientists review how young people around the world have used social media to improve the political situation in their countries. The authors, Yousri Marzouki and Olivier Oullier, write that Twitter and Facebook have significantly empowered large, like-minded groups to bring about social and political change. Social networking spurred the Arab Spring revolutions that started in 2010, including a change of regime in Tunisia and Egypt. The authors report on a study they conducted on the role of Facebook in political revolution and explain that leaderless revolutions have been made possible by cyberactivism. Yousri Marzouki is an associate professor of psychology and Olivier Oullier a professor of behavioral and brain sciences at Aix-Marseille University in France.

Discussions about the influence of social media often [bring to mind] those on the impact of TV in the 1980s: Everyone has an opinion, some have statistics, and a few others are trying to understand the psychological and sociological mechanisms that lie beneath.

Activists in downtown Cairo, Egypt, check Twitter updates on November 27, 2011, the day before Egyptian elections. Social media played an important role in that country's revolution earlier that year.

The incredible connectivity amongst people that is provided by social media, combined with the speed at which information is exchanged and its potential global reach, have significantly empowered people. One way to have an estimate of this empowerment is to look at how users managed to "hijack" some social media platforms from their initial use. Twitter and Facebook users provide a spontaneous snapshot of their individual states of minds but, unintentionally, they also turn them into an incredible tool for collective estimates of behavioral dynamics . . . and crowdsourcing. Facebook . . . is on its way to reaching the billion-user landmark and has already changed the way more than 10 percent of the people on this planet interact with each other as revealed by a rich body of research in social sciences. Some people, including the founders of Twitter and Facebook, might have anticipated for all of this to happen. But did they expect the role social media play not only in igniting revolutions but also in modifying how regime change is achieved?

Cyber-Activism and the Arab Spring

Think about what history will now remember as the Arab Spring. This recent [2010–2013] wave of revolutions has yielded some successful and significant regime changes including, so far, Tunisia, Egypt, Libya and Yemen. One year after, established social movements' theories fall short in explaining how both the Tunisian and the Egyptian revolutions occurred. One reason is the influence of cyber-activism via social media platforms that classical approaches to collective movements do not take into account. Indeed, these two successful popular uprisings are marked by the absence of a clearly identified leader, a political party or figure, an association, or an organizing capacity.

Instead of a leader that would have inspired people and driven them to start—and achieve—a revolution, Facebook was the main channel that facilitated and accelerated the Tunisian revolution as repeatedly reported in the news and by many observers. Twitter, too, played a crucial role during the Egyptian revolution. Hence, it is very likely that without these social networking platforms, these revolutions would certainly have evolved more slowly, if at all, and would have never reached the global opinion.

But Twitter and Facebook were not ghosts in the machine. They were "just" catalysts to these emerging patterns of popular uprisings. They allowed not only to speed up information exchange but also to provide unprecedented waves of spread. A recently published study that was launched five days after the fall of the [Tunisian president] Ben Ali regime and led by our team at Aix-Marseille University & CNRS [the National Center for Scientific Research (France)] provides a novel "cyberpsychological" take on how Tunisian Internet users perceive the contribution of Facebook to their 2011 revolution. The method is

Virtual Collective Consciousness (VCC)

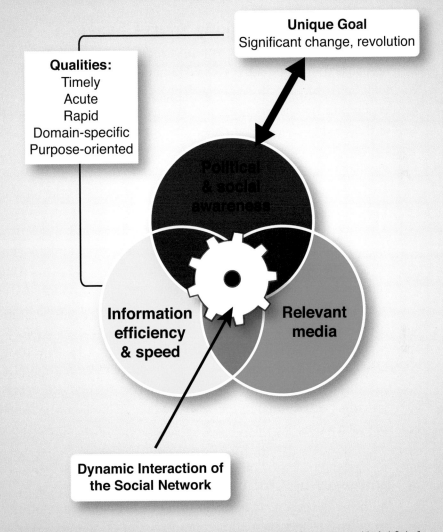

Unique Goal
Significant change, revolution

Qualities:
Timely
Acute
Rapid
Domain-specific
Purpose-oriented

Political & social awareness

Information efficiency & speed

Relevant media

Dynamic Interaction of the Social Network

Taken from: Yousri Marzouki and Olivier Oullier, "Revolutionizing Revolutions: Virtual Consciousness and the Arab Spring," *Huffington Post*, May 22, 2014. www.huffingtonpost.com.

pretty straightforward. After analyzing a sizeable text corpus from Tunisian Internet users' responses to an online questionnaire, three main clusters were extracted corresponding to what were labeled Facebook's (1) political function, (2) informational function and (3) media platform function.

How Social Networking Spurs Change

This study provides a bottom-up approach to these new social uprisings that relied on virtual environments instead of the dominant top-down accounts of "classical revolutions" powered by leaders pulling strings. Accordingly, the interpretation of the results of this study lies on a complex dynamical system by invoking the concept of emergent behavior. Indeed, the complex interconnectivity between individuals involved in the revolutionary process within the Tunisian Facebook cyber-activism network—and the Twitter one in Egypt—yields patterns of accumulating change.

Hence, the possibility of a leaderless revolution is likely to be (at least partially) explained by the spontaneity, the homogeneity and the synchronicity of the actions of these cyber-activism networks that were catalyzed by social media. This explanation is supported by what we coined virtual collective consciousness (VCC) referring to an internal knowledge shared by a plurality of persons. Coupled with "citizen media" activism, this knowledge emerges as a new form of consciousness via communication tools. . . . Accordingly, VCC has to be: timely, acute, rapid, domain-specific and purpose-oriented, which are potential "qualities" of a successful movement (see figure).

Empowering Ordinary Citizens

With the deepening of globalization in the 21st century, the new geopolitical landscape allows a new vision of democracy where ordinary citizens might be more empowered than ever before to choose an alternative system and change policies. Carne Ross anticipated such global citizen behavior months before the Arab Spring burst out. In his manifesto *The Leaderless Revolution: How*

Ordinary People Will Take Power and Change Politics in the 21st Century, he provides nine principles on how ordinary citizens can regain control of the decisions that directly impact their lives. We support the idea that these principles should be federated around a global consensus shared by citizens.

One of the lessons to be learned from the Arab Spring is that a new breed of revolutions, henceforth called leaderless revolutions, has started, driven by VCC and facilitated by social media. This does not mean that leaders cannot play a significant role in such contexts. Only that, with social media as catalysts, they are no longer a *sine qua non* condition to successful regime changes.

Virtual collective consciousness afforded by social media might have very well revolutionized revolutions.

TWELVE

Social Networking Is Not Real Activism

Mark Kersten

The following viewpoint is the text of a debate speech delivered by Mark Kersten, a criminal justice professor, at the Oxford Union, a debate society founded at Oxford University in England. The topic of the debate was whether social media has successfully reinvented social activism. Kersten argues that it has not. He argues that social networking has been critically important to a number of so-called Twitter revolutions in the Middle East, as well as in social campaigns such as the *Kony2012* video, but, Kersten contends, society is just beginning to understand how and whether social networking can produce lasting, real-life results. The author passionately argues that activists are real people working in actual communities and that cyberactivism cannot replicate or replace their role. Mark Kersten teaches international political theory and genocide studies at the London School of Economics. He is the creator and a coauthor of Justice in Conflict, a website that focuses on the political aspects of justice in ongoing conflicts and on conflicting conceptions of justice.

There is no point in . . . denying that social media has changed how political and social activism is done. It clearly and obviously has. Despite this, social media has not, I will argue, "reinvented" the fundamental rules of social activism. To suggest so is to misunderstand what it means to do social activism and to be a social activist.

We are told a very simple story about the relationship between social media and social activism. You have all heard it. Social media topples Arab tyrants. Social media leads to democratic elections. Social media can bring rebel leaders in the heart of Africa to justice. At the core of this apparently irresistible narrative is the belief that social and political campaigns are a success when they achieve massive online traffic and "go viral". The problem here is simple. None of the above is true.

An absolutely necessary condition for the effectiveness and success of a social campaign is building a political community of real-life, off-line physical human beings committed to a common cause.

Key Examples of Cyber-Activism

Take for example, Invisible Children's KONY2012 campaign [to raise awareness of atrocities by Joseph Kony and the Lord's Resistance Army in central Africa]. It did not go viral randomly or because of celebrity endorsements on Twitter and Facebook. Beneath this popular veneer, is the reality that Invisible Children worked for almost a decade to build a network of like-minded individuals willing to drive across Canada and the United States in order to show the group's latest films in schools and churches. It should thus come as no surprise that KONY2012 began trending on Twitter before the campaign video itself was released—as the carefully cultivated community of Christian youths in mid-sized American cities began tweeting.

Consider too, the role of social media in the Arab Spring. It would be wrong to attribute the effectiveness and success of human rights and democracy campaigners in Egypt, Tunisia, Libya, Bahrain, and so on, entirely to social media. The opposition to these regimes had learned from decades of experience, training in human rights and civil disobedience.

The people who bravely marched on Tahrir Square in Cairo and Green Square in Tripoli did so not because they heard about

Kony2012: The Most Viral Video in History

Number of days to 100 million views:

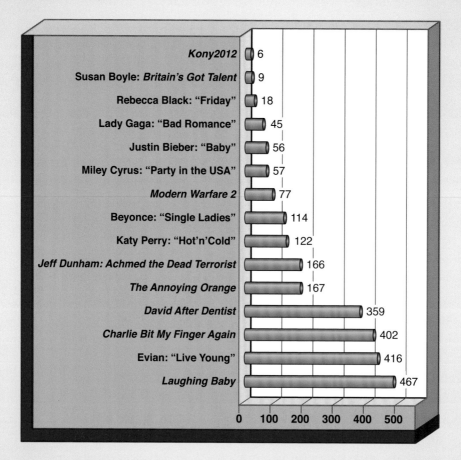

Kony2012	6
Susan Boyle: *Britain's Got Talent*	9
Rebecca Black: "Friday"	18
Lady Gaga: "Bad Romance"	45
Justin Bieber: "Baby"	56
Miley Cyrus: "Party in the USA"	57
Modern Warfare 2	77
Beyonce: "Single Ladies"	114
Katy Perry: "Hot'n'Cold"	122
Jeff Dunham: Achmed the Dead Terrorist	166
The Annoying Orange	167
David After Dentist	359
Charlie Bit My Finger Again	402
Evian: "Live Young"	416
Laughing Baby	467

Taken from: "Update: Kony Social Video Campaign Tops 100 Million Views," Visible Measures, March 12, 2012. www.visiblemeasures.com.

it on Twitter but because of real grievances; because of years of outrage and humiliation; because, to them, enough was enough.

Part of the popular narrative also tells us that re-tweeters and sharers on Facebook themselves are a new breed [of] social activists, ready at the whim to tackle tyranny and oppression, their iPads and iPhones proof of their commitment to liberal democratic values. Of course, they're not the same type of activists. Instead, the popular and rather disparaging argument is that they are "slactivists". Again, this is fundamentally misleading. Sharing and re-tweeting KONY2012 was a symbolic action, the merits of which we can debate. But it was symbolic action taken almost exclusively by people who were never activists in the first place. This helps to explain why Invisible Children's campaign to "Cover the Night"—which required real activists—was such an epic flop.

Activists Are Real People in Actual Communities

It bears repeating: it is the communities of real people on the ground who are the activists. They are the ones who confront, challenge and sometimes alter the very social and political fabric of their societies by making long-term commitments, making personal sacrifices and often putting themselves at risk. Twitter and Facebook haven't reinvented what they do. They have been doing it for years, sometimes decades before Twitter and Facebook even existed! Rather, we must understand that in this age of persuasion, social media is one of the tools available to social activists. But when social media is effectively employed in campaigns, it remains the activists, revolutionaries and dissidents who deserve the credit for challenging the status quo—and not social media itself.

In short, tweets and facebook statuses don't topple dictators and they don't capture international criminals. Troublingly, the belief that they do may reveal a very uncomfortable truth in how we view the social and political struggle of others.

Consider that the vast majority of tweets during Iran's "Twitter Revolution" were made from outside Iran, by people in the West and in English. Indeed, only 20,000 people in Iran in 2009 used Twitter, a paltry 0.00025% of the population! Consider too that

KONY2012's implicit message that the way to resolve the suffering of an entire region of Africa lies in the capacity of American students to share a video through social media and make Joseph Kony famous.

Online Activists Do Virtually Nothing

The common denominator, it seems to me, is that we retain a desire to *own* the change and the ability of distant others to take matters into their own hands, even when we do virtually nothing—and retweeting is just that—to affect it. It is this self-reflexive view which drives the narrative that Twitter, Facebook,

A protester demonstrates during the Arab Spring revolution in Tunisia in January 2011. Critics contend that real activists are people who effect change directly within their communities.

and the other social media we use, creates the change we want to see in Iran, Central Africa, and the Arab world. There thus exists a profound risk that, in attributing agency to platforms like Twitter and Facebook, we strip agency from precisely those activists who have sacrificed and taken risks to achieve it in the first place.

Social media is, of course, a double-edged sword, used by undemocratic and repressive forces to plant farcical stories, stifle debate, monitor the masses and track activists. Sadly, these practices are often propped up software and tech groups in Western, democratic countries. As others have shown, an open Internet and social media does not necessarily lead to democracy or transparency—it can act to strengthen authoritarian regimes rather than weaken them.

Nevertheless, social media can be an incredibly powerful tool. Events like the Arab Spring would not have garnered as much international attention nor spread so rapidly had it not been for the effective use of social media by activists. What previously may have taken them years to achieve can now take days, hours or even minutes. But let us celebrate the possibility and potential of social media by being honest about its role and limitations.

Social Media Cannot Reinvent Real Change

The fact remains: social media cannot reinvent what it means to do social activism, to be political, and to achieve social change. Social media platforms remain a necessary but insufficient condition for effective social and political activism.

I'll leave you with this. When, in 10 or 20 years time, we look back on the Arab Spring, will we attribute the causes and dynamics of the revolutions to Twitter, Facebook or blogs or will we respect that the upheavals and gains were achieved because of *real* people, in *real* communities, in *real*-time, with *real* grievances working to effect *real* change? I think it will be the latter. It should be the latter. And I hope so, too.

What You Should Know About Social Networking

Facts About Social Networking

- Online social networks make it possible for people who share interests and activities to connect across political, economic, and geographic borders.
- Seventy-four percent of adults online use social networking sites.
- Ninety-eight percent of eighteen- to twenty-four-year-olds use social media.
- Seventy-one percent of online adults use Facebook; 19 percent use Twitter; 17 percent use Instagram; 21 percent use Pinterest; and 22 percent use LinkedIn.
- Seventy-four percent of women use social networking sites, compared with 62 percent of men.
- Between February 2005 and August 2006, the use of social networking sites among young adult Internet users aged eighteen to twenty-nine jumped from 9 percent to 49 percent.
- Forty percent of mobile phone owners use a social networking site on their phone, and 28 percent do so on a typical day. Young people, blacks, Hispanics, the highly educated, and those with a higher annual household income are more likely to use social networking sites on their phones than are other groups.
- Forty-six percent of adult Internet users post online photos or videos that they created; 41 percent of adult Internet users

take photos or videos that they have found online and repost them on social networking sites.

- People in the following countries spend the most hours per month on social networking: Israel (11.1 hours), Argentina (10.7 hours), Russia (10.4 hours), Turkey (10.2 hours), and Chile (9.8 hours). Americans spend an average of 7.6 hours per month on social media.
- In 2013, people aged fifty-five to sixty-four were the fastest-growing demographic on Twitter. The number of users in this age bracket has grown by 79 percent since 2012. On Facebook and Google+, the forty-five to fifty-four age bracket is the fastest-growing demographic, having grown 46 percent for Facebook and 56 percent for Google+.
- Ninety-three percent of marketers say they use social media for business.

Facts About Social Networking Safety and Privacy
- Fifty-nine percent of teens view social networks as unsafe.
- Sixty percent of teen Facebook users keep their profiles private, and most say they are confident in their ability to manage privacy settings.
- Ninety-one percent of teens report posting a photo of themselves online.
- Seventy-one percent of teens post their school name online and 71 percent have posted the city or town where they live.
- Fifty-three percent of teens say they post their e-mail address online, and 20 percent say they post their cell phone number.
- To help protect their privacy, 26 percent of teens say that they post false information online, such as a fake name, age, or location.
- Nearly 43 percent of kids have been bullied online, and 70 percent of students report seeing frequent bullying online.
- Girls are about twice as likely as boys to be victims as well as perpetrators of cyberbullying.
- Compared with teens who spend no time on social networking sites in a typical day, teens that do are five times likelier

to use tobacco, three times likelier to use alcohol, and twice as likely to use marijuana.

Facts About Social Networking Services

As of July 2014,

- Facebook
  - had 1.4 billion users worldwide—about 11 percent of the world's population.
  - users share 1 million links every twenty minutes.
  - had 189 million "mobile only" users.
  - privacy settings are ignored by about 25 percent of users.
- YouTube
  - had more than 1 billion visitors each month.
  - users watched more than 6 billion hours of video every month.
  - reached more US adults between the ages of eighteen and thirty-four than any cable TV network.
- Twitter
  - had 241 million active users (and more than 600 million total users).
  - had fifty-seven hundred tweets uploaded every second.
- Instagram
  - had 200 million active users.
  - statistics showed that 57 percent of US users visited the site at least once a day, and 35 percent did so multiple times a day.
- Google+
  - had 540 million active users.
  - users that were most active on the service were twenty-five- to thirty-five-year-olds.
- LinkedIn
  - had 300 million users.
  - analysts claimed that 50 percent of the job hires worldwide used its site.
- Pinterest
  - had 20 million active users and 70 million total users.
  - users were 17 percent male and 83 percent female.

What You Should Do About Social Networking

You have rights and responsibilities as a member of a social networking site. Be aware of both the risks and the benefits of social networking. Be nice, be safe, and have fun.

Your actions online have personal and ethical implications and could have real-world consequences for you, your family, and your friends. Consider the potential consequences before you post a picture or video, upload a comment, or send a message.

Learn all you can about the privacy settings of each social networking service you use, and protect your personal information.

It is impossible to completely control who will see your profile, pictures, videos, and texts after they have been uploaded to the Internet. Consider how you might feel if your family, teachers, coaches, or neighbors—as well as school recruiters and potential employers—would see your social networking activity.

Keep it positive and polite. Treat others as you would like to be treated. Use your social network feed and posts to boost your friends' morale and to promote a culture of civility.

Before you post a photo or video of someone else, get permission. Remember they have privacy and other concerns to consider, just as you do.

Speak up if you see or experience bullying or something inappropriate on a social networking site. Let the site know (by using the "report abuse" feature, for example) and tell an adult you trust.

Do not impersonate other people.

Explore new interests and be open to and tolerant of the opinions of those different from you. Social networking can greatly expand your perspective on the world and your life.

The editors have compiled the following list of organizations concerned with the issues debated in this book. The descriptions are derived from materials provided by the organizations. All have publications or information available for interested readers. The list was compiled on the date of publication of the present volume; the information provided here may change. Be aware that many organizations take several weeks or longer to respond to inquiries, so allow as much time as possible for the receipt of requested materials.

Common Sense Media
650 Townsend Street, Suite 435
San Francisco, CA 94103
(415) 863-0600 • fax: (415) 863-0601
www.commonsensemedia.org

Common Sense Media provides informational and educational media and technology to improve the lives of kids and families. It conducts research to provide parents, educators, organizations, and policy makers with data on children's use of media and technology and the impact it has on their physical, emotional, social, and intellectual development. Reports such as *Social Media, Social Life: How Teens View Their Digital Lives*, and *Children, Teens, and Entertainment Media: The View from the Classroom* are available on its website.

DoSomething.org
19 W. 21st Street, 8th Floor
New York, NY 10010
(212) 254-2390
www.dosomething.org

DoSomething.org is one of the largest organizations for young people and social change. Its 2.6 million members create and tackle campaigns that impact causes important to teens, such as poverty, violence, the environment, and animals. Members can create projects for any cause and which are then searchable by cause, amount of time required, and type of activity, including action through social networks. The organization also sponsors scholarships and awards.

Gay, Lesbian and Straight Education Network (GLSEN)
90 Broad Street, 2nd Floor
New York, NY 10004
(212) 727-0135 • fax: (212) 727-0254
e-mail: glsen@glsen.org
website: www.glsen.org

Founded in 1990 and established nationally in 1995, GLSEN fosters healthy, safe school environments where every student is respected regardless of sexual orientation. It is the oversight organization of more than four thousand school-based Gay-Straight Alliances (GSAs) and the sponsor of two antidiscrimination school events, the National Day of Silence and No Name-Calling Week. The GLSEN website offers research reports such as *From Teasing to Torment: School Climate in America; A National Report on School Bullying; Shared Differences: The Experiences of Lesbian, Gay, Bisexual, and Transgender Students of Color;* and *Out Online: The Experiences of Lesbian, Gay, Bisexual and Transgender Youth,* the first national, in-depth report of the LGBT youth experience online.

National Crime Prevention Council (NCPC)
2345 Crystal Drive, Suite 500
Arlington, VA 22202
(202) 466-6272 • fax: (202) 296-1356
website: www.ncpc.org/topics/cyberbullying

The council, a partnership of the US Department of Justice and private sponsors such as the Wireless Foundation and the Ad Council, was founded in 1979 to get citizens, especially youth, involved in crime prevention. It is best known for televised public service announcements and school-based programs featuring

McGruff the Crime Dog. Its website includes a section on Internet safety and offers antibullying banners users can copy and paste into e-mails or social networking pages.

Pew Internet and American Life Project
1615 L Street NW, Suite 700
Washington, DC 20036
(202) 419-4300 • fax: (202) 419-4349
www.pewinternet.org

The Pew Research Center's Internet and American Life Project is a comprehensive source of information on the evolution of the Internet through surveys that examine how Americans use the Internet and how these activities affect their lives. The project conducts nationwide random phone surveys, online surveys, and qualitative research and releases fifteen to twenty reports each year. Its website includes fact sheets and infographics and access to reports such as *Teens, Social Media, and Privacy* and *Social Media and Mobile Internet Use Among Teens and Young Adults*.

Protect My Rep
University of St. Thomas
2115 Summit Ave., Mail 5057
Saint Paul, MN 55105-1096
(651) 962-5282
e-mail: threesixty@stthomas.edu
www.protectmyrep.org

Protect My Rep informs teens about social media use and aims to place social media privacy and Internet safety at the forefront of teens' minds. It encourages users to use #protectmyrep on Facebook, Twitter, and Instagram to share what they have learned and mistakes they have made with social networking. Its website includes sections such as "Social Media 101," "Who's Watching," and "How to Protect Yourself." The tips, reports, and information available on the website help teens become safer and savvier users of the Internet. Protect My Rep is a project of ThreeSixty Journalism, a Minnesota teen journalism program by teens for teens, sponsored by the University of St. Thomas.

US Department of Education

400 Maryland Ave. SW
Washington, DC 20202
(800) 872-5327
website: www.ed.gov

The US Department of Education promotes student achievement and preparation for global competitiveness by fostering educational excellence and ensuring equal access to education. It establishes policies related to federal education funding, administers and monitors the use of funds, collects data and oversees research on US schools, identifies major issues in education, and enforces federal laws prohibiting discrimination in programs that receive federal funding. The department publishes a variety of newsletters on specific topics relating to education, and its website includes a section on social networking tools.

Wired Safety

1 Bridge Street
Irvington-on-Hudson, NY 10533
(201) 463-8663
website: www.wiredsafety.org

Wired Safety is an Internet safety and help group that offers articles, activities, and advice designed for seven- to seventeen-year-olds on a range of issues, including cyberbullying, cyberstalking, and harassment. Resources include a Cyber911 Help Line, a cyberstalking poll, cyberbullying Q&As, and a speakers bureau. Information available on the website covers Facebook privacy protection, how to handle sexting, building safe websites, and other topics. Wired Safety also sponsors a cyberbullying website called Stop Cyberbullying at www.stopcyberbullying.org.

BIBLIOGRAPHY

Books

Nancy K. Baym, *Personal Connections in the Digital Age*. Malden, MA: Polity, 2010.

Tina Bettison, *Social Networking for Rookies: From Rookie to Expert in a Week*. London, UK: LID, 2014.

Howard Gardner, *The App Generation: How Today's Youth Navigate Identity, Intimacy, and Imagination in a Digital World*. New Haven, CT: Yale University Press, 2013.

Lori Hile, *Social Networks and Blogs*. Chicago: Raintree, 2011.

Laurie Collier Hillstrom, *Online Social Networks*. Detroit: Lucent, 2010.

Carla Mooney, *Online Social Networking*. Detroit: Lucent, 2009.

Jennifer Obee, *Social Networking: The Ultimate Teen Guide*. Lanham, MD: Scarecrow, 2012.

Lee Rainie and Barry Wellman, *Networked: The New Social Operating System*. Cambridge, MA: MIT Press, 2012.

Corey Sandler, *Living with the Internet and Online Dangers*. New York: Checkmark/Facts On File, 2010.

Tom Standage, *Writing on the Wall: Social Media—the First 2,000 Years*. New York: Bloomsbury, 2013.

Adam Sutherland, *The Story of Facebook*. New York: Rosen, 2012.

Sherry Turkle, *Alone Together: Why We Expect More from Technology and Less from Each Other*. New York: Basic Books, 2011.

Periodicals and Internet Sources

Elizabeth Blair, "Online, Researcher Says, Teens Do What They've Always Done," an interview with danah boyd, National Public Radio, February 25, 2014. www.npr.org.

Libby Copeland, "The Anti-social Network: By Helping Other People Look Happy, Facebook Is Making Us Sad," *Slate*, January 26, 2011. www.slate.com.

Marcia DeSanctis, "Prof Sherry Turkle Interview for *In Real Life*," *The Telegraph* (UK), September 9, 2013. www.telegraph.co.uk.

Megan Garber, "Saving the Lost Art of Conversation," *The Atlantic*, December 22, 2013.

Malcolm Gladwell, "Small Change: Why the Revolution Will Not Be Tweeted," *New Yorker*, October 4, 2010.

Nicholas D. Kristof, "After Recess: Change the World," *New York Times*, February 4, 2012.

Ethan Kross and Philippe Verduyn, "Facebook Use Predicts Declines in Subjective Well-Being in Young Adults," *PLoS One*, August 13, 2013.

Gwenn Schurgin O'Keeffe, Kathleen Clarke-Pearson, and Council on Communications and Media, "The Impact of Social Media on Children, Adolescents, and Families," *Pediatrics*, April 2011.

Pew Internet and American Life Project, "Social Networking Fact Sheet," September 2013. www.pewinternet.org.

Pew Internet and American Life Project, "Teens, Social Media, and Privacy," May 21, 2013. www.pewinternet.org.

Michael Price, "Alone in the Crowd," *Monitor on Psychology*, June 2011.

Larry D. Rosen, "Poke Me: How Social Networks Can Both Help and Harm Our Kids," American Psychological Association, 2011 Annual Convention, Fenichel's Current Topics in Psychology. www.fenichel.com/pokeme.shtml.

Rita Safranek, "The Emerging Role of Social Media in Political and Regime Change," ProQuest Discovery Guides, March 2012. www.csa.com/discoveryguides/social_media/review.pdf

Hilary Stout, "Antisocial Networking?," *New York Times*, May 1, 2010.

Kaveri Subrahmanyam, and Patricia M. Greenfield, "Online Communication and Adolescent Relationships," *Children and Electronic Media*, Spring 2008. http://futureofchildren.org.

Marcos Suliveres, "Social Media: The Death of Real World Interaction," Medium.com, July 15, 2014. https://medium.com.

Sherry Turkle, "Connected, but Alone?," TED Talk transcript, April 2012. www.ted.com/talks/sherry_turkle_alone_together/transcript#t-734000.

Website

OnGuard Online (www.onguardonline.gov). OnGuard Online is the federal government's website to help Americans be safe, secure, and responsible online. The Federal Trade Commission manages the site in partnership with the Department of Homeland Security, the US Department of Education, and other federal agencies. The website provides access to a number of free publications and resources on how to avoid scams, understand mobile apps, and create secure wireless networks. There are also special materials for families and young people about online safety.

INDEX

Delinquent behaviors, 54
Duke University, 5
Dustin, Samuel, 35

E
Egypt, 7, 76, 81–82
  See also Arab Spring
Egyptian Day Against Homo-
  phobia (EDAHO), 72
Egyptian LGBT community,
  70, 72
ELIZA (computer program),
  16
Everyday Sexism Project,
  63–65

F
Facebook
  civil rights and, 73
  Egyptian LGBT activism
    and, 72
  inaccurate identities on, 29
  LGBT activism on, 69
  phenomenon of, 5, 31
  political change with, 74–79,
    84–85
  relationship status on, 23
  social connections with, 40
  social good on, 13–14
  teen expression on, 35
  victim-blaming comments
    on, 55–56
Family life and technology,
  20–21
Formspring.me, 61–62, 65
Friedman, Ann, 55–60
Friedman, Nancy, 14

Friendships, online connections and, 11, 20, 25–26, 39,
  41
Friendster, 5
Furby (toy), 16

G
Genovese, Kitty, 58, 59n1
Geocities, 5
Glasionov, Esther, 66–73
Goffman, Erving, 26, 28–29
Gram, Sarah, 59
Grimm, Lisa, 32–33, 35
Grow Global Citizens (Face-
  book group), 13

H
Hage, Rita, 66–73
Harvard University, 5
Hess, Amanda, 57
Hodkinson, Paul, 26
Human Rights Campaign
  (HRC), 69
Humphrey, Katie, 33

I
The Independent (newspaper),
  63
Instagram
  parental monitoring of, 11
  teen expression on, 35
  video-sharing function, 6,
    32, 33
Invisible Children (organization), 7, 81, 83
Iran, 83–85

PICTURE CREDITS